AUTONOMY
IN THE LAW

IUS GENTIUM
COMPARATIVE PERSPECTIVES ON LAW AND JUSTICE

VOLUME 1

Series Editor

Mortimer Sellers
(University of Baltimore)

Board of Editors

AUTONOMY

IN THE LAW

16100

Edited by

MORTIMER SELLERS

 Springer

A C.I.P. Catalogue record for this book is available from the Library of Congress.

ISBN 978-1-4020-6489-0 (HB)
ISBN 978-1-4020-6490-6 (e-book)

Published by Springer,
P.O. Box 17, 3300 AA Dordrecht, The Netherlands.

www.springer.com

Printed on acid-free paper

To the Student Fellows of the Center for
International and Comparative Law,
past, present and future,
with gratitude and affection.

CONTENTS

PREFACE

The collection of essays in this volume is first in the series *Ius Gentium: Comparative Perspectives on Law and Justice*, published by Springer Verlag in cooperation with the University of Baltimore Center for International and Comparative Law. This book series replaces the journal *Ius Gentium*, which concluded with volume 12 in 2006.

The essays in this collection are based on papers originally presented at the fifth meeting of the European-American Consortium for Legal Education (EACLE), held at American University in Washington, D.C. in May, 2006. EACLE has published several previous collections of essays in the journal *Ius Gentium*. For a list of past volumes, see http://law.ubalt.edu/cicl/ilt.

EACLE is a transatlantic consortium of law faculties dedicated to cooperation and the exchange of ideas between different legal systems and cultures. Each year the EACLE colloquium considers a specific legal question from a variety of national perspectives. The 2006 initiative on "Autonomy" was coordinated by Professor Robert Dinerstein of the American University School of Law.

I would like to thank those who attended the 2006 meeting for their insightful remarks, and for their inspiration, suggestions, and encouragement in making this volume and the EACLE consortium so effective in fostering greater transatlantic cooperation on law and legal education.

Thanks are also due to the faculty, staff and students of the Center for International and Comparative Law who prepared this volume for publication, and particularly to Morad Eghbal, James Maxeiner, Kathryn A. Spanogle, Natalie J. Minor, Renee L. Bailey, P. Hong Le, Thomas Pilkerton III, David Schaffer, Pooja Shivangi, Katherine Simpson, Catherine Wahl, Ryan Webster and Cheri Wendt-Taczak.

Mortimer Sellers
Baltimore, Maryland

NOTES ON CONTRIBUTORS

June Carbone is the Edward A. Smith/Missouri Chair in Law, the Constitution and Society at the University of Missouri-Kansas City.

Tessa Gombeer is an Assistant in the Department of Criminal Law and Criminology at the University of Ghent.

Jan Klabbers is the Director of the Center of Excellence in Global Governance Research and Professor of International Organizations Law at the University of Helsinki.

Marc A. Loth is the Dean of the Faculty of Law at Erasmus University Rotterdam.

Kandis Scott is Professor of Law at Santa Clara University School of Law.

Mortimer Sellers is Regents Professor of the University System of Maryland and the Director of the University of Baltimore Center for International and Comparative Law.

Philip Traest is Professor of Criminal Law at the University of Ghent.

An Introduction to the Value of Autonomy in Law

M.N.S. Sellers

Autonomy has universal appeal, but vastly divergent applications in different legal systems and in different circumstances. Like all legal ideals, legal embodiments of the value of autonomy must seek generality in principle, to justify particularly in practice. When lawyers from different jurisdictions compare their differing doctrines, this comparison clarifies what all legal systems have in common, or ought to have in common. The value of autonomy can be discovered in the overlapping ideals of otherwise dissimilar legal systems, in which conceptions of autonomy shape the structures of relationships between individuals and their families, between families and the state, and between the state and international organizations. Concerns for autonomy determine how lawyers may defend their clients, and what clients can expect from their lawyers. Each of these circumstances reveals a different conception of autonomy, and the ultimate unity of the underlying concept that informs them all. Protecting autonomy is one of the central benefits of law.

Autonomy, in its simplest and most natural sense, signifies self-rule: the right of states, or of families, or of associations or individuals to make their own laws for themselves. Understood in this way, autonomy is almost a synonym for license, which is to say, the ability to do what one wants, without restraint. Autonomy differs from license, however, in that it implies some measure of self-restraint. This difference is not in itself enough to justify the concept's popularity. What makes autonomy so desirable is its inevitable connect-

1

ion with (and restraint by) liberty, understood as the right not to be interfered with by the state or by others, except to the extent that this interference is warranted by the common good of society as a whole. Liberty, so defined, is among the most important purposes and justifications of law. Law draws the lines that protect the autonomy of states, of families, and of persons, from the unwarranted intrusions of other persons, families, the state, or anyone else.

Law protects liberty and the autonomy of various groups by drawing the lines that determine the range of their self-rule. This makes autonomy itself an inevitable product of law. Autonomy is not only an inevitable, but also a desirable result of legality, because liberty (and, therefore, some measure of autonomy) is a central element in justice. If justice consists (as it does) in those social arrangements that best maintain and advance the common good of all members of society, and true justice is achieved in a state or society when all its members have the opportunity to lead worthwhile and fulfilling lives, then liberty and autonomy are essential prerequisites of justice, because worthwhile lives require some element of self-rule. If law seeks justice (as it should), then law will protect liberty, and autonomy will always be a central element in law.

The importance of autonomy in law is also intimately connected with the concept of privacy, which guards individuals, families and associations against unwarranted intrusion. "Privacy" is the negative expression of the positive value expressed by "autonomy." Autonomy signifies the right to decide for oneself. Privacy signifies that zone in which no others may interfere. Both privacy and autonomy are fundamental requirements in any just legal order because they both are basic attributes of liberty, and liberty is a fundamental element of the common good that all legal systems have a basic obligation to establish and protect.[1]

---

[1] *See* M.N.S. Sellers, *Republican Legal Theory*. Macmillan, Basingstoke, 2003.

Liberty is the assurance that individual autonomy (privacy) will not be invaded, unless the common good of the people as a whole warrants this invasion.[2]

Privacy is best understood as comprising that zone in which individuals ought to enjoy autonomy. Some actions are private in the sense that they are the activities in which the state ought not to take an interest. The state ought not to constrain its subjects in their private activities, because these arise, by definition, only when citizens ought to enjoy autonomy. Those activities in which the state could legitimately constrain autonomy constitute the public sphere. Personal autonomy properly ends at the boundary between the public and the private. This boundary is determined in turn by the areas in which individuals (or groups) ought or ought not to enjoy autonomy.

These definitions of law, justice, liberty and the common good are not (or at least ought not to be) controversial. They have been well-established for centuries. But the concept of autonomy is more complicated, largely because of the influence of Immanuel Kant. Kant believed in the possibility of a sort of false consciousness in which a person desires or intends one thing, but really would (or should) have wanted something else, if only the person were reasonable, and thought clearly.[3] Kant perceived that persons in the grip of an unregulated passion or desire or emotion, may make wrong choices. So neo-Kantians now often speak of "moral autonomy," to signify the choices that people would make if they were not so short-sighted and morally obtuse. Kant advocated moral autonomy only insofar as it signifies doing the right things for the right reasons. This way of looking at things is very similar to the attitude of Jean-Jacques Rousseau,

[2] See M.N.S. Sellers, *The Sacred Fire of Liberty*. Macmillan, Basingstoke, 1998.

[3] Immanuel Kant, *Critique of Pure Reason*, translated and edited by Paul Guyer and Allen Wood. Cambridge, 1997.

who wrote of "forcing" people to be free.[4]

This conception of autonomy does violence to our ordinary use of language. The better and more usual understanding of autonomy restricts itself to what is sometimes called "personal autonomy": the opportunity to regulate one's own life for oneself, according to one's own judgment, even when one's judgment is bad. The proper zone of personal privacy is that area in which a person ought to be able to regulate her or his own life, according to her or his own judgment, even when that judgment is wrong.

This understanding of autonomy recalls the basic premises with which this discussion began. Law, for example, exists to secure justice, as much as it possibly can, but there may be some elements of justice that cannot be secured by law, or should not be. In the just distribution of pieces of cake at a party, for example, the person who cuts the cake should strive for a just distribution of cake, but the common good would suffer if societies tried to secure the just distribution of cake by force of law. This is equally true of the just distribution of chores within a family. Families properly enjoy a certain amount of autonomy. But, as this example shows, autonomy should have limits, because it can facilitate oppression. Families can become oppressive, and so the state properly imposes limits on their autonomy, in order to prevent oppression within families. The autonomy of some actors must be constrained when it begins to threaten the common good of the whole.

When we speak of autonomy, or of privacy, or of self-rule, we can speak of the privacy or autonomy or self-rule of individuals, and what limits we should place on these to facilitate the common good of the whole. But we can also speak of the privacy or autonomy or self-rule of groups. For example, families, churches, nations, or regions can enjoy

---

[4] "On le forcera à être libre" Jean-Jaques Rousseau, *The Social Contract* I.7.8, translated and edited by Victor Gourevitch. Cambridge, 1997.

autonomy, as can many other organized groups. Groups can maintain a private or autonomous sphere, within which they enjoy independence, even while they are also subject to broader bodies of law, which constrain their autonomy and prevent them from oppressing others. This is as it should be. Discussions of autonomy must always recur to this question of precisely where to draw the line between the "public" and the "private" spheres, to better define the area in which individuals, or organizations, or states ought to have autonomy, and those areas in which they ought to be subject to external control.

This comparison between individuals and groups gives rise to several possible areas of confusion about autonomy and privacy as applied to law. There are important differences between individual and collective self-rule. Individuals benefit directly from liberty. We all properly enjoy and benefit from being able to regulate our own lives (subject to constraints placed upon us for the common good). Oppression arises from constraints imposed for reasons unrelated to the common good. Such oppression is a great human misery, both because it hurts to have one's will arbitrarily thwarted and because one's own plan for one's own welfare is usually more effective than choices imposed by others. So individuals should enjoy autonomy and ought to have some measure of self rule. But groups are different from individuals in this respect. A group's title to self-rule is entirely derivative from the welfare of the individuals within it and of other members of society as a whole, because groups cannot have a single autonomous will or judgment, as individuals do. It is, therefore, necessarily often the case that when groups make decisions, the autonomy of particular members of the group will be overruled. This makes the process by which groups make decisions extremely important. Decisions must be made for the good of the community as a whole, not for the separate good of dominant elites or of self-serving individuals within larger groups of people.

The first question to be asked in evaluating group autonomy should be whether the group itself is useful and whether it serves the common good of its members and of society as a whole. Criminal gangs should enjoy a much narrower zone of autonomy, for example, than the Roman Catholic church; and the Roman Catholic church should have more limited autonomy that the State of Maryland. Group autonomy should depend on the purposes for which the group exists and how well the group actually serves these purposes. People sometimes confuse democracy with autonomy, for example, but this overlooks the fact that in democracies individuals can be outvoted, to the detriment of their own personal autonomy, and therefore run the risk of being oppressed.

Another common confusion about autonomy arises from mistaking personal failings for external controls. This was Kant's mistake. Autonomy is not directly compromised when individuals make bad choices. In fact, the essence of autonomy is the ability to make bad choices for oneself. Good choices are demeaned when they are not freely chosen.

The third common mistake about autonomy is to imagine that autonomy is always desirable. There are a great many bad choices that people ought not to be allowed to make, because they have such dangerous consequences. The effects of one's actions on others will often justify some measure of constraint.

The concept of privacy also gives rise to some common confusions. Many mistakenly believe that any public interest trumps all private rights. But sometimes privacy properly protects violations of the public good. Protecting the borders of personal autonomy may require very broad rules that provide a shield for bad behavior. Privacy also has a territorial as well as a behavioral component. My autonomy has a greater importance in my home, for example, than it does on the public street, where I am more likely to come into contact with others.

A second common mistake about privacy would be to

suppose that private desires always deserve public support. The common good does not necessarily embrace all private desires. A just legal system will tolerate some forms of private behavior that it does not and should not actively support.

These distinctions and similarities between autonomy, privacy, liberty, and license, as applied to law, become more apparent in the context of their application to particular cases and circumstances. For example, as June Carbone demonstrates in this volume, the autonomy to construct one's own family has primary importance in the lives of most people, whose most intimate relationships are perpetuated and supported by family bonds. On the other hand, children born into families have no such autonomy, and deserve legal protection against the self-interest of other family members.

International organizations are much more remote from everyday life, but they too have the power both to liberate, by constraining national governments and to oppress, by interfering in individual lives. Jan Klabbers explains how important procedural checks and balances will be in guiding international organizations, both toward exercising their own autonomy properly and toward respecting the autonomy of others. International organizations have a legitimate zone of autonomous action, as do states, and corporations, and individuals. The difficulty arises in drawing the lines of autonomy and control within and between these different actors.

Nowhere does autonomy seem more important than the decision to end one's own life. Both capital punishment and assisted suicide cases turn on this question of life and death and our hesitancy to permit the purposeful ending of human life, even when death is freely chosen. Kandis Scott suggests that people should have the autonomy to end their own lives, when their considered judgment finds the conditions of life to be intolerable and there is no remedy for their suffering. Mark Loth adds that even the creation of a life may violate autonomy, when parents wish to prevent a birth, and fail.

When poor medical advice leads to the unwanted birth of profoundly handicapped children, different courts in different jurisdictions have imposed different underlying rules. Yet no matter which rule is ostensibly chosen, the final legal result is often the same. This reflects universal standards of personal autonomy and justice which confer legitimacy on the courts, and constrain court decisions, to reach substantively just results.

Procedural justice also concerns autonomy, since it protects zones of privacy and self-expression against the operations of the courts. Philip Traest and Tessa Gombeer explain how the rights of the defense in legal proceedings extend to counsel, and how the legal autonomy of lawyers advances the liberty rights of their clients. The defense counsel is in a sense an extension of the legal personality of the defendant and should therefore retain considerable autonomy against the court. At the same time, counsel cannot and should not be held liable for the crimes of those they (legally) undertake to defend. Any restrictions on attorney/client privilege undermine the autonomy which even actual wrongdoers should retain in undergoing the judicial application of the law.

These practical examples of the implications of autonomy for law can be supplemented with some specific observations about the legal system of the United States. The United States Constitution guarantees that neither the Federal government nor any state can deprive any person of life, liberty, or property, without due process of law. This has been interpreted to mean that there are certain liberties that cannot rightfully be denied. These constitute a perpetually private zone, into which the state can never intrude. So the United States Constitution protects for each citizen a zone of autonomy, concerning his or her own body, above all, but also his or her house, private opinions, and religious views, to give just three examples. This empowers judges to constrain the government and legislature, in order to protect individual citizens against arbitrary power. Many lawyers consider this to be the most important provision of the United States Constitution. By referring directly to liberty, the Constitution embeds justice and the common good at the heart of the constitutional structure, and guarantees a zone of privacy and autonomy to all citizens, so that they can enjoy the blessings of liberty, not only against each other, but also against the state.

Privacy, autonomy and liberty are all three closely related to the republican and liberal foundations of justice under law. Law should seek to establish justice for all, which requires both the imposition of restraints for the common good and the protection of individual and group autonomy, so that each citizen can be in a sense the author of her of his own life, with the protection and support of the state, the law, and society as a whole. Autonomy is one of the most important benefits and justifying purposes of the rule of law.

Autonomy To Choose What Constitutes Family: Oxymoron Or Basic Right?

June Carbone

Alasdair MacIntyre, Michael Sandel, and other critics have argued that liberalism is living off the borrowed capital of Western civilization.[1] That is, to the extent that liberalism requires neutrality among theories of the good, the generation of values – of strong families, hard workers, honest people, engaged citizens, and devout church members – takes place offstage. These critics worry that the institutions that develop values, such as churches and families, have atrophied in the modern secular state, and that liberalism can no longer assume that private institutions will serve the purposes that, before the rise of liberalism, had been advanced by the state.[2]

William Galston responded to this critique by arguing that liberalism does not require neutrality toward the creation of the values that are central to liberalism itself.[3] A liberal

---

[1] See Alasdair Macintyre, *After Virtue* (2d ed. 1984); Michael J. Sandel, "Introduction," in Michael J. Sandel, ed, *Liberalism and Its Critics* (NYU, 1984), at 5; Michael J. Sandel, *Democracy's Discontent* (1996), at 7-8. For a summary of this debate within family law, see Jennifer Wriggins, "Marriage Law and Family Law: Autonomy, Interdependence, and Couples of the Same Gender," 41 *B.C. L. Rev.* 265 (2000), at 265-67 (summarizing discussion, including Bruce Hafen, Carl Schneider, and Mary Ann Glendon, about the law's expressive function and the communitarian critique of individualism).

[2] See, e.g., *Reynolds v. United States*, 98 U.S. 145, 162 (1879) (noting that the colonies sometimes required church attendance and used tax dollars to support established churches).

[3] William A. Galston, *Liberal Purposes: Goods, Virtues, and Diversity in the Liberal State* (1991), at 220-21. *See also* Stephen Macedo, *Liberal Virtues: Citizenship, Virtue, and Community in Liberal Constitutionalism* (1990), at 200.

democratic state should be able to foster "liberal virtues" such as tolerance, industry, honesty, family stability, and civic engagement. Indeed, historically, liberal states have strongly regulated sexual morality, family stability, and educational quantity and content.

This raises the question, how a liberal state can promote such values in the absence of consensus not just on the values themselves, but on the institutions necessary to inculcate them. The United States today, for example, deals with differences in educational philosophies by allowing parents and students to choose among public or private schools, established schools or home schooling.[4] The relationship between church and state similarly involves a long and tortured effort to balance free expression, which necessarily requires a measure of autonomy in creating religious institutions, and the establishment clause, which mandates state neutrality among the institutions created.

Some issues, however, require that the state make choices. Traffic regulation is an easy example; drivers cannot construct rival roadways, some of which mandate driving on the left and others on the right. The choice of a democracy over a monarchy provides another illustration. A state may recognize an individual's right to express a preference for a monarchy over a democracy without giving the individual a right to be governed by a monarch or to opt out of the requirements of democratic governance. In these cases, the autonomy of the individual to choose one institution over another is necessarily limited.

The question that is emerging today is whether state regulation of the family is such an area. Historically, the idea of autonomy with respect to the creation of family form would have been considered an oxymoron to the extent

---

[4] Indeed, the United States has enjoyed a healthy debate both on the most effective form of educational institutions (comprehensive public schools versus niche designed charter schools, vouchers to subsidize public schools, etc.) and the extent of state power to compel attendance. *See, e.g., Wisconsin v. Yoder*, 406 U.S. 205 (1972).

that the issue arose at all. The traditional family of biological mother, father, and child was often treated as prior to the state,[5] if not foundational to society itself.[6] The Supreme Court has recognized marriage as "an institution, in the maintenance of which in its purity the public is deeply interested, for it is the foundation of the family and of society, without which there would be neither civilization nor progress."[7] Nor has the state been neutral among the possible forms of marriage. When the Supreme Court confronted the issue of polygamy as an expression of Mormon religious practice in the Utah territories during the nineteenth century, it had no trouble declaring "the organization of a community for the spread and practice of polygamy is, in a measure, a return to barbarism. It is contrary to the spirit of Christianity and of the civilization which Christianity has produced in the Western world."[8]

The basis for these decisions, for the denial of autonomy with respect to the choice of institutions, and not just individual behavior, bears revisiting. As an initial matter, the Supreme Court has distinguished between belief and practice. The First Amendment protects the former, but not necessarily the latter.[9] That distinction holds today, especially with

---

[5] *See, e.g.,* Paul Peachey, "Family, Society & State in the USA: Some Reflections" in *Private and Public Social Inventions in Modern Societies* (Paul Peachey, Leon Dyczewski, & John Kromkowski, eds.), available at http://www.crvp.org/book/Series04/IVA-2/chapter_iv.htm ("Conventionally we view the family as prior to the society, both genetically and historically; genetically, because the family provides the human material from which the state and other social formations are constructed; historically, because as we well know the family precedes the state.").

[6] *See, e.g., Loving v. Virginia*, 388 U.S. 1, 12 (1967) (finding marriage "fundamental to our very existence and survival").

[7] Maynard v. Hill, 125 U.S. 190, 210-211 (1888).

[8] *Late Corp. of the Church of Jesus Christ of Latter-Day Saints v. United States*, 136 U.S. 1, 48-49 (1890).

[9] *Reynolds*, 98 U.S. at 166, observing that:

Suppose one believed that human sacrifices were a necessary part of religious worship,

respect to a practice that is permitted, but not compelled, by one's religion.[10] Second, in determining whether the state could regulate practice, the Court has considered the existence of consensus, consensus based on factors that shift over time. In the nineteenth century, for example, the Court explicitly acknowledged the United States' legacy as a nation of European immigrants, stating bluntly that "[p]olygamy has always been odious among the northern and western nations of Europe, and, until the establishment of the Mormon Church, was almost exclusively a feature of the life of Asiatic and of African people."[11] More fundamentally, however, the Court went on to examine the basis for the preference of monogamy over polygamy. It concluded that:

> Upon... [marriage] society may be said to be built, and out of its fruits spring social relations and social obligations and duties, with which government is necessarily required to deal. In fact, according as monogamous or polygamous marriages are allowed, do we find the principles on which the government of the people, to a greater or less extent, rests. Professor Lieber says, polygamy leads to the patriarchal principle, and which, when applied to large communities, fetters the people in stationary despotism, while that principle cannot long exist in connection with monogamy.[12]

---

would it be seriously contended that the civil government under which he lived could not interfere to prevent a sacrifice? Or if a wife religiously believed it was her duty to burn herself upon the funeral pile of her dead husband, would it be beyond the power of the civil government to prevent her carrying her belief into practice?

[10] *See, e.g., Smith v. Fair Empl. & Hous. Comm'n*, 913 P.2d 909 (Cal. 1996) (holding that a landlord cannot refuse to rent to unmarried intimate partners whose behavior violates the landlord's religious beliefs because nothing in the landlord's religious beliefs requires the landlord to be in the business of renting apartments).

[11] *Reynolds*, 98 U.S. at 164.

[12] *Id.* at 165-66 (citations omitted). The Court stated further: "An exceptional colony of polygamists under an exceptional leadership may sometimes exist for a time without appearing

The state could accordingly choose one institution (monogamy) over another (polygamy) where that choice reflected both the consensus views of the populace and the promotion of values (liberty and equality over despotism) consistent with a democracy.

This reasoning leaves open the obligation of the state over the choice of basic institutions where these conditions do not hold. What if, on questions basic to the organization of family, no consensus exists? What if different demographic and economic circumstances create different family traditions among different states? What if fundamentally different values in different parts of the country produce polarization rather than agreement on the family values appropriate for a liberal democracy? Does the state obligation to recognize autonomy in the selection of family form change?

This paper will address these issues by, first, examining the debate about the regulation of morality and distinguishing the control of individual behavior from the selection of basic institutions. Second, it will examine the polarization now taking place on the definition of family values among the states and argue that these differences reflect different challenges produced by the nature of the interaction among marriage, childbearing, and the adult life cycle. Third, it will maintain that these differences, while the product of different approaches to family institutions consistent with historic efforts at secular family regulation, interact with religious, as well as secular beliefs. Finally, the paper will consider what some measure of autonomy and respect for others might entail in a system in which different states adopt fundamentally different approaches toward the definition and regulation of family values.

The paper will conclude that in an era of polarization the

---

to disturb the social condition of the people who surround it; but there cannot be a doubt that, unless restricted by some form of constitution, it is within the legitimate scope of the power of every civil government to determine whether polygamy or monogamy shall be the law of social life under its dominion." *Id.* at 166.

state cannot remain neutral in the choice of basic values, and it should be able to choose, on a majoritarian basis, to promote one set of values over another. Autonomy in the constitution of family as a state-sanctioned status thus becomes impossible. In these circumstances, the obligation of a liberal state then becomes one of minimizing the "moral affront" to the views of the rejected minority, and preserving individual autonomy in the expression of contrary views or private conduct.

1. THE REGULATION OF SEXUAL MORALITY

The regulation of individual behavior is distinct from the regulation of institutions. Nonetheless, the two are related and even in liberal states committed to individual autonomy, some regulation of sexual morality has been the norm. The question of whether that regulation can be reconciled with individual liberty has generated centuries of discussion.[13] Perhaps the classic debate within the Anglo-American tradition occurred between Patrick Devlin and H.L.A. Hart in the nineteen-fifties. A British Parliamentary Committee had proposed deregulating sexual behavior between consenting adults, and repealing the laws that criminalized, among other things, homosexuality and prostitution. Lord Devlin opposed the liberalization on two grounds. He argued, first, that every society has the right to conserve its own traditions, to preserve the practices that are distinctive to its culture,[14] and, second, that a society must preserve its fundamental morality in order not to disintegrate.[15]

---

[13] Some would date the Anglo-American discussion to John Stuart Mill and his work entitled *On Liberty*. *See* Robert C.L. Moffat, "Commentary: 'Not The Law's Business:' The Politics Of Tolerance And The Enforcement Of Morality," 57 *Fla. L. Rev.* 1097 (2005), at 1098.

[14] Patrick Devlin, *The Enforcement of Morals* (1972), at 11.

[15] *Id.* at 10 ("[W]ithout shared ideas on politics, morals, and ethics no society can exist..... If men and women try to create a society in which there is no fundamental agreement about good and

Devlin would judge a society's fundamental morality in terms of those acts that a jury of representative citizens would find offensive. Michael McConnell defends this deference to a communal or consensus based moral view in terms not so different from the Supreme Court's nineteenth century deference to "Western civilization." Professor McConnell argues that:

> An individual has only his own, necessarily limited, intelligence and experience (personal and vicarious) to draw upon. Tradition, by contrast, is composed of the cumulative thoughts and experiences of thousands of individuals over an expanse of time, each of them making incremental and experimental alterations (often unconsciously), which are then adopted or rejected (again, often unconsciously) on the basis of experience—the experience, that is, of whether they advance the good life.[16]

H.L.A. Hart responded to Devlin (and implicitly to McConnell's identification of the source of Devlin's morality) by questioning whether any notion of morality can be determined with certainty, and whether change over time could be said to produce the "disintegration" of society. He observed that Devlin's argument moved "from the acceptable proposition that some shared morality is essential to the existence of any society to the unacceptable proposition that a society is identical with its morality as that is at any given moment of its history, so that a change in its morality is tantamount to the destruction of a society," and called the latter proposition "absurd."[17]

---

evil they will fail; ...the society will disintegrate.").

[16] Robin West, "Progressive And Conservative Constitutionalism," 88 *Mich. L. Rev.* 641 (1990), at 654-55.

[17] H. L. A. Hart, *Law, Liberty, and Morality* (1963), at 51,52. He continued: "Taken strictly, it

As Hart emphasizes, part of the challenge for those who would regulate morality is to identify the possibilities for change. Must the Aztecs, for example, continue to honor human sacrifice or the United States take the position that the racial segregation deeply rooted in its traditions cannot be changed?[18] Just as fundamental for the Hart/Devlin debate is the notion of harm. Mill originated the idea of harm to others as the principal justification for state regulation of individual conduct.[19] At what point can private consensual behavior between adults be said to affect anyone else?[20] Perhaps the best answer for Devlin is Professor Jeffrie Murphy's. "[O]ne might... argue," Professor Murphy suggested, "that open toleration of the flouting of sexual norms threatens the honorific position historically accorded the traditional nuclear family and that such a threat risks undermining the social stability generated by such family units."[21] If individuals do not have an obligation to resist "temptation," if those around them engage in "sin" without condemnation or consequences, then the internalized norms of fidelity and commitment will atrophy, and a higher percentage of the next generation's children will be raised in suboptimal circumstances. Devlin's position, as Murphy suggests, is that the internalization of shared norms is simultaneously fragile and fundamental to the society implementing it. Nonetheless, it is still important to determine whether particular moral precepts remain "shared" or "fundamental" over time.

---

would prevent us saying that the morality of a given society had changed, and would compel us instead to say that one society had disappeared and another one taken its place. But it is only on this absurd criterion of what it is for the same society to continue to exist that it could be asserted without evidence that any deviation from a society's shared morality threatens its existence." *Id.* at 52.

[18] Moffat, *supra* note 13, at 1104.

[19] *See supra* sources from note 13.

[20] Moffat, *supra* note 13, at 1102.

[21] Jeffrie G. Murphy, "Legal Moralism and Liberalism," 37 *Ariz. L. Rev.* 73 (1995), at 77.

The Supreme Court's decision in *Lawrence v. Texas*,[22] overturning Texas's criminal ban on same-sex sodomy, would appear to answer that at least for now the public attitude toward private sexual behavior between consenting adults has changed. Poll data supports the conclusion of a widespread change in attitudes. The Gallup organization has polled American adults since 1977, asking whether they believe that homosexual activity should be criminalized and compiled the following results:

Date	Legal (%)	Not Legal (%)	No Opinion (%)
1977-JUN	43	43	14
1982-JUN	45	39	16
1985-NOV	44	47	9
1986-JUL	32	57	11
1986-SEP	33	54	13
1987-MAR	33	55	12
1988-JUL	35	57	11
1989-OCT	47	36	17
1992-JUN	48	44	8
1996-NOV	47	47	9
1999-FEB	50	43	7
2001-MAY	54	42	4
2002-MAY	52	43	5
2003-MAY	60	35	5

These poll results show a substantial shift in attitudes over time, with 60 percent favoring the legalization of such behavior before the Supreme Court ruled on the issue in 2003.[23]

---

[22] 539 U.S. 558 (2003).

[23] Available at http://www.religioustolerance.org/hom_poll2.htm (asking "Do you think homosexual relations between consenting adults should or should not be legal?"). Both the majority and dissenting opinions in Lawrence acknowledged the changing sentiment. Kennedy observed that "later generations can see that laws once thought necessary and proper in fact serve only to oppress." *Lawrence*, 539 U.S. at 579. Scalia responded "and when that happens, later generations can repeal those laws." *Id.* at 604 (Scalia, J., dissenting).

The scholarly debate over *Lawrence* has focused less on the outcome, and more on the question of whether Justice Kennedy's majority opinion simply declared such intimate behavior to be beyond the scope of legitimate government intervention, or went further to affirm the value and dignity of same-sex relationships.[24] The majority opinion, acknowledging the "powerful voices" condemning homosexuality as immoral, nonetheless emphasized that the "...issue is whether the majority may use the power of the State to enforce these views on the whole society through operation of the criminal law. 'Our obligation is to define the liberty of all, not to mandate our own moral code.'"[25] Kennedy's opinion underscored "the respect the Constitution demands for the autonomy of the person in making these choices," and cited the abortion cases to reiterate that:

> These matters, involving the most intimate and personal choices a person may make in a lifetime, choices central to personal dignity and autonomy,

---

[24] *See* David D. Meyer, "Domesticating *Lawrence*," 2004 *U. Chi. Legal F.* 453 (2004), at 466; Marybeth Herald, "A Bedroom of One's Own: Morality and Sexual Privacy After *Lawrence v. Texas*," 16 *Yale J.L. & Feminism* 1 (2004), at 30, ("*Lawrence* is also clear that the case did 'not involve whether the government must give formal recognition to any relationship that homosexual persons seek to enter.' Thus, same-sex marriage and military service were explicitly excluded from the ruling."), Martin R. Gardner, "Adoption by Homosexuals in the Wake of *Lawrence v. Texas*," 6 *J. L. & Fam. Studs.* 19 (2004), at 43, ("There is good reason to disagree, however, with Justice Scalia's conclusion that *Lawrence* will inevitably lead to a constitutional requirement of homosexual marriages."). *See also* Nelson Lund & John O. McGinnis, "*Lawrence v. Texas* and Judicial Hubris," 102 *Mich. L. Rev.* 1555 (2004), at 1583 (criticizing Lawrence as a wrong-headed extension of substantive due process and wondering whether "something resembling the Playboy Philosophy will become the official doctrine of the United States"); *cf.* Katherine M. Franke, "The Domesticated Liberty of *Lawrence v. Texas*," 104 *Colum. L. Rev.* 1399 (2004), at 1417 ("Sex gets figured, if at all, in Lawrence as instrumental to the formation of intimate relationships-it seems not to have a social or legal status in its own right. As a result, sexual rights qua sexual are exiled from the legal struggle on behalf of gay men and lesbians."); Mark Strasser, "Monogamy, Licentiousness, Desuetude and Mere Tolerance: The Multiple Misinterpretations of *Lawrence v. Texas*," 15 *S. Cal. Rev. L. & Women's Stud.* 95 (2005) (summarizing different views and concluding that *Lawrence* should be seen as affirming gay, lesbian, and other non-traditional relationships).

[25] *Lawrence*, 539 U.S. at 571.

are central to the liberty protected by the Fourteenth Amendment. At the heart of liberty is the right to define one's own concept of existence, of meaning, of the universe, and of the mystery of human life. Beliefs about these matters could not define the attributes of personhood were they formed under compulsion of the State.[26]

Justice Scalia's dissenting opinion castigates the majority for having "taken sides in the culture war."[27] Although Kennedy emphasized that the case did not address "whether the government must give formal recognition to any relationship that homosexual persons seek to enter,"[28] Scalia responded:

More illuminating than this bald, unreasoned disclaimer is the progression of thought displayed by an earlier passage in the Court's opinion, which notes the constitutional protections afforded to "personal decisions relating to *marriage*, procreation, contraception, family relationships, child rearing, and education," and then declares that "persons in a homosexual relationship may seek autonomy for these purposes, just as heterosexual persons do."[29]

Lawrence, precisely because of its emphasis on privacy, leaves open the larger issue of the role of moral regulation in a democracy. The state, after all, rarely polices consensual sexual behavior between adults, whether or not the conduct is legal; it routinely regulates the creation and dissolution of families. Decisions about which relationships to recognize

---

[26] *Planned Parenthood of S.E. Pa.* v. *Casey,* 505 U.S. 833, 851 (1992).

[27] *Lawrence,* 539 U.S. at 602 (Scalia, J., dissenting).

[28] *Id.* at 578.

[29] *Id.* at 604. (Scalia, J., dissenting) (emphasis in original).

and which to ignore, which factors to recognize in custody
decisions, and which family members to protect all involve
moral judgments.[30] In addition, while Hart argues persuasively
that the "disintegration" that might be associated with private
sexual conduct is too tangential a harm to justify punitive
measures, the constitution and conduct of families affects
children – often directly – and almost always as part of a
social compact that establishes the bases on which children
receive support.

The question accordingly arises: is Scalia right? Does Kennedy's recognition of autonomy with respect to "personal decisions relating to marriage, procreation, contraception, family relationships, child rearing, and education"[31] necessarily
mean that a liberal state must also recognize autonomy to
create and win state recognition for the institutions necessary to implement such personal decisions?

2. THE POLARIZATION OF FAMILY VALUES

2.1 *The Redefinition of Family Values*

While the regulation of family institutions (e.g., recognition
of marriage, divorce, and parentage) is distinct from the
regulation of sexual conduct, both have historically rested
on the same values. Chancellor Kent, for example, in his
summary of American law at the beginning of the nineteenth
century, observed that:

> The primary and most important of the domestic
> relations is that of husband and wife. It has its
> foundations in nature, and is the only lawful relation
> by which Providence has permitted the continuance

---

[30] Naomi R. Cahn, "The Moral Complexities of Family Law," 50 *Stan. L. Rev.* 225 (1997).

[31] *Lawrence*, 539 U.S. at 574.

of the human race. In every age it has had a propitious influence on the moral improvement and happiness of mankind. It is one of the chief foundations of the moral order. We may justly place to the credit of the institutional of marriage a great share of the blessings which flow from the refinement of manners, the education of children, the sense of justice, and cultivation of the liberal arts.[32]

For Kent, the relation of "husband and wife" was a legal one separate from that of biological mother and father. It had its "foundations in nature" in that marriage provided a providentially mandated way to channel the natural inclinations arising from sex and reproduction.[33] It served, moreover, not just as the foundation of the moral order, but also as a principal way to secure the "education of children," a "sense of justice," and other practical ends important to a well functioning state. Accordingly, a major purpose of domestic relations law was to distinguish between properly constituted versus illicit relations. Sexual morality and family regulation were intricately intertwined.

Modern critics, in contrast, have charged that contemporary family law no longer serves to promote marriage as the foundation of the moral order. These criticisms have two components. First, a series of scholars, starting with Carl Schneider, claim "a diminution of the law's discourse in moral terms about the relations between family members, and the transfer of many moral decisions from the law to the people the law once regulated."[34] Moral values, and the promotion of

---

[32] James Kent, 2 *Commentaries on American Law* (12th ed., Oliver Wendell Holmes, Jr., ed., Boston: Little Brown, 1896), at 76.

[33] *See, e.g.,* Stephen J. Pope, "Sex, Marriage and Family Life: The Teachings of Nature," in *Family Transformed: Religion Values, and Society in American Life* (Steven M. Tipton & John Witte, Jr., eds., 2005), at 65.

[34] Carl E. Schneider, "Moral Discourse and the Transformation of American Family Law," 83 *Mich. L. Rev.* 1803 (1985), at 1808-09. *See also* Bruce C. Hafen, "The Family as an Entity,"

the conduct associated with them, have become the province of private institutions and individual actors rather than the state. A second group maintains that the state, while it may endorse some values, fails to promote the right ones. These advocates maintain, "that traditional families—two parent, heterosexual married couples with children—are essential to a healthy society and must be encouraged."[35] What the critics have largely not considered is the possibility that the states, entrusted in the American federal system with primary responsibility for the regulation of family law, may be adopting not only different, but incompatible systems.

Family law scholars have, however, charted the emergence of a set of values different from those Chancellor Kent championed. Naomi Cahn, for example, argued almost a decade ago that a newly evolving morality recognized responsibility for children as a familial obligation, albeit with public support, made gender equity a "primary objective," and placed individual rights "within the contexts of community, equality, and commitment."[36] Jane Murphy seconded the idea, maintaining that there is a "broader concept of morality" that emphasizes the "virtues of care and protection of children"

---

22 *U.C. Davis L. Rev.* 865 (1989), 879 ("state intervention into family life... is less likely now than previously to be based on moral judgments"); Jana B. Singer, "The Privatization of Family Law," 1992 *Wis. L. Rev.* 1443 (1992), at 1527 (arguing that the "increased dissociation of law and morality... is directly linked to the privatization of family law"); Lee E. Teitelbaum, "The Last Decade(s) of American Family Law," 46 *J. Legal Ed.* 546 (1996), at 547 (noting a decline in moral discourse in some areas of family law).

[35] Jane C. Murphy, "Rules, Responsibility And Commitment To Children: The New Language Of Morality In Family Law," 60 *U. Pitt. L. Rev.* 1111 (1999), at 1113 (summarizing debate and arguing that in fact family law promotes a different and more appropriate set of values). *See also* Judith E. Koons, "Motherhood, Marriage, And Morality: The Pro-Marriage Moral Discourse Of American Welfare Policy," 19 *Wis. Women's L. J.* 1 (2004), at 23 (summarizing the argument of marriage advocates that "over the past forty years there has been an 'extraordinary shift in cultural norms concerning sex, marriage, and childbearing,' including the advent of birth control, the entry of more women into the labor force, and the increasing acceptability of cohabitation outside of wedlock . . . . Widened opportunities for women, including alternatives to marriage, that were the fruits of the women's and civil rights movements are constitutive of this normative shift.").

[36] Cahn, *supra* note 30, at 270-71.

and addresses "issues that are more commonly thought of as economic or psychological issues, such as how to guarantee adequate support for children and how to evaluate parental fitness."[37]

This alternative set of family values, with its emphasis on care and support for children, draws as much on Anglo-American tradition as the model that rests on sexual regularity. Lawrence Stone, in his history of the family in England, emphasized the relatively high portions of the population who never married, and the relatively late marital age for those who did, as "an extraordinarily and unique feature of northwest European civilization."[38] Stone explained that while in some parts of the world newlyweds remained with their parents, the English tradition (and that of northwestern Europe more generally), emphasized the ability to establish a financially independent household as the indication of readiness for marriage. Moral responsibility meant financial, as well as sexual restraint in preparation for parenthood.

In similar fashion, a shift in investment strategies produced a transformation in family norms in the nineteenth century United States, with industrialization, the professions, and the executive ranks replacing farms and shops as the most secure avenues to middle class status. Prescient families began to invest more in their sons' formal education and daughters' virtue, and to keep their growing children more carefully supervised in the home. As a result, the average age of marriage rose, the number of births per family fell, women gained greater status as the guardians of family virtue,[39] greater

---

[37] Murphy, *supra* note 35, at 1204.

[38] Lawrence Stone, *The Family, Sex and Marriage in England, 1500-1800* (abridged ed. 1979), at 44.

[39] *See* Jane E. Larson, "Women Understand So Little, They Call My Good Nature 'Deceit': A Feminist Rethinking Of Seduction," 93 *Colum. L. Rev.* 374 (1993), at 388 ("Victorian culture exalted sexual restraint and designated women as caretakers of society's sexual virtue."). Larson also notes, however, that: "Although the Victorian convention of female sexual modesty repressed women's sexuality, it also strengthened women's social authority and dignity,

condemnation attended engagement-period intercourse, and pregnancy rates fell from one-third of brides to ten percent by mid-century.[40] The Protestant middle class remade "family values" and celebrated their moral superiority to the detriment of Catholic immigrants, freed slaves, and others who could not afford to keep women and children insulated from temptation.[41] These values, firmly cemented within the northwest European tradition to which Americans are heirs, continued to herald financial independence and investment in children as hallmarks of family morality.

The twentieth century's post-industrial economy further remade the family bargain. The rise of the service sector increased demand for women's market services, and rewarded greater investment in women. Women then reorganized themselves, as higher earning women hired others to provide the less specialized services they had once performed within the home. As women joined men in securing higher education, the new path to secure middle class status lay in delayed marriage and childbearing for women as well as men.

---

empowering women to resist male sexual demands and thus shifting the balance of power between men and women in the private sphere." *Id.* at 389-90.

[40] *See* Carl N. Degler, *At Odds: Women and the Family in America from the Revolution to the Present* (1980), at 9, 180-83 (on declining birth rates that followed women's greater ability to decline sexual intercourse); Linda Hirshman & Jane Larson, *Hard Bargains: The Politics of Sex* (1998) (The number of women giving birth within eight and a half months of marriage fell from thirty percent at the end of the eighteenth century to ten percent by the middle of nineteenth century).

[41] For a discussion of the class and racial aspects of these developments, see June Carbone, *From Partners to Parents: The Second Revolution in Family Law* (2000), at 108-110. *See also* Larson, *supra* note 39 at 388 n. 55 (observing that, "The separate spheres ideology largely applied to white, middle-class, heterosexual women. Although society measured women outside this category against these feminine ideals of sexual purity and domesticity (often to their detriment), more marginalized women were rarely accorded the moral authority and social respect which the separate spheres ideology implied that all women deserved. *See*, e.g., Elizabeth Fox-Genovese, *Within the Plantation Household: Black and White Women of the Old South* (1988), at 192-241 (describing gulf between slaveholding and enslaved women in the antebellum American South); Jacqueline Jones, *Labor of Love, Labor of Sorrow: Black Women, Work, and the Family from Slavery to the Present* (1985), at 1-151 (comparing experience of free and enslaved black women in southern United States).").

Ironically, the new movement grew out of the nineteen-fifties in which all of the trends that had otherwise characterized the twentieth century reversed themselves. Stephanie Coontz writes that "[f]or the first time in more than one hundred years, the age for marriage and motherhood fell, fertility increased, divorce rates declined, and women's degree of educational parity with men dropped sharply."[42] The solution was the contraceptive pill in the nineteen-sixties, abortion in the nineteen-seventies, and the effective disappearance of the norms of sexual restraint for adult singles. By 1997, the Gallup poll found that fifty-five percent of American adults say that premarital sex is not wrong, and among the most directly affected, *viz.*, younger Americans aged 18-29, 75 percent agreed that "pre-marital sexual relations are not wrong."[43] The new middle class separated sex and childbearing; improvident childbearing could still derail a woman's education, marriage, and income prospects, while the former had become available without stigma or commitment.[44]

As with the nineteenth-century changes, the twentieth century changes in women's status and independence changed the terms on which they were willing to enter into and stay in marriages. Stephanie Coontz comments that:

> As women gained experience and self-confidence, they won benefits that made work more attractive and rewarding; with longer work experience and greater

---

[42] Stephanie Coontz, *The Way We Never Were: American Families and the Nostalgia Trap* (1992), at 202-03.

[43] Frank Newport, "Gallup Poll Review From The Poll Editors: Sexual Norms: Where Does America Stand Today?," *The Gallup Poll* (December, 1997), available at http://www.hi-ho.ne.jp/taku77/refer/ sexnorm.htm.

[44] Whitehead notes that ninety percent of women born between 1933 and 1942 were either virgins when they married or had their first experience of sexual intercourse with the man they later married. Today, in contrast, the average age of first intercourse for women is seventeen while the average age of first marriage is twenty-five. Barbara Dafoe Whitehead, "The Changing Pathway to Marriage: Trends in Dating, First Unions, and Marriage among Young Adults," in Tipton & Witte, *supra* note 33, at 170.

educational equalization, they became freer to leave an unhappy marriage; and as divorce became more of a possibility, women tended to hedge their bets by insisting on the right to work. Although very few researchers believe that women's employment has been a direct cause of the rising divorce rate, most agree that women's new employment options have made it easier for couples to separate if they are dissatisfied for other reasons. In turn, the fragility of marriage has joined economic pressures, income incentives, educational preparation, and dissatisfaction with domestic isolation as one of the reasons that modern women choose to work.[45]

The economic coercion that complemented the moral suasion of the older family system gave way, and so did the effectiveness of the mechanisms that promoted family stability for centuries.

As Cahn and Murphy emphasized, however, the results are not entirely unhappy ones. The new middle class morality emphasizes the financial contributions of mothers and fathers, and it celebrates marriage in terms of equality and companionship. While the research evidence on marital happiness is mixed, there are many reasons to believe that the most troubled adults have become less likely to marry or stay married, those who rate their relationships fair or equitable are more likely to stay together, and two incomes have become critical to families' financial well-being for all but the wealthiest Americans.[46] The middle class may see no alterna-

---

[45] Coontz, *supra* note 42, at 166.

[46] *See, e.g.,* John M. Gottman, et al., "Predicting Marital Happiness and Stability from Newlywed Interactions," 60 *J. Marriage & Fam.* 5 (1998) (stating men's rejection of their wives' influence best predicts divorce); Kristi Williams, "Has the Future of Marriage Arrived? A Contemporary Examination of Gender, Marriage, and Psychological Well-Being," 44 *J. Health & Social Behavior* 470 (2003), at 487 (individuals are better divorced than in unhappy marriages). *But see* Robert Wurthnow, "The Family as Contested Terrain," in Tipton & Witte, *supra* note 33, at

tive to the strategy of later, more egalitarian marriages – at least on the East and West coasts of the United States.

The families in a large part of the rest of the country, however, are in crisis. The combination of the atrophy of the traditional constraints on sexual behavior with the difficulty of engineering the new middle class ideal of companionate relationships has undermined the conventional links between adult resources and support for children. For the country as a whole, non-marital births have risen to a third of the total. Divorce rates have risen steadily from 5 percent of marriages in 1867, to 10 percent in 1900, to half in 1967, and perhaps as many as two-thirds of those who married in 1980.[47] Half of American children can expect to live in a single parent family at some point in their childhood, and the outcomes for children in single parent families are demonstrably worse on a host of measures than for those in married families. Moreover, some scholars argue that even though more troubled adults have become less likely to marry, the quality of marital happiness has not risen. Robert Wurthrow, for example, cites poll data that shows 62.4 percent of married couples claiming to be very happy in 2000 compared to 67.8 percent in 1973.[48] And these issues do not play out evenly across the country. Instead, they divide by race, income, education – and geography. The "blue" states, that is, the states that voted for the Democratic candidate in the 2004 presidential election, show the lowest rates of teen pregnancy, divorce, and poverty, while the "red" states, which voted Republican in the last election, show the highest rates of improvident teen births and divorce.

---

74 (summarizing evidence of greater unhappiness of those currently married in comparison with earlier areas, and greater well-being of the married compared to the unmarried).

[47] Wurthrow, *supra* note 46, at 74 (noting that while divorce rates have leveled off more recently, the change is due in part to the fact that fewer couples are marrying. Any effect of greater self-selection today may not necessarily be reflected in those married in 1980).

[48] *Id.* at 74.

The "red states" also believe they have an answer – a much higher percentage of their populations would say "no" to the new middle class morality of unregulated sex and egalitarian marriage. Instead, they would embrace a more traditional, and more religiously grounded, definition of family morality. Critical to that definition is the unity of sex, marriage, and reproduction. A recently released letter from the Religious Coalition for Marriage, for example, explains:

> Marriage is particularly important for the rearing of children as they flourish best under the long term care and nurture of their father and mother. For this and other reasons, when marriage is entered into and gotten out of lightly, when it is no longer the boundary of sexual activity, or when it is allowed to be radically redefined, a host of personal and civic ills can be expected to follow.[49]

The marriage movement, which has been more influential in red states than blue ones,[50] would accordingly advocate greater emphasis on the distinction between licit and illicit sex, greater commitment to marriage, and reaffirmation of the importance of the biological two-parent family.

In addition, many of the researchers supporting these movements believe that traditional notions of family and a gendered division of family responsibilities are critical to the outcome. All researchers report that women are more likely than men to initiate divorce, and that women's emotional satisfaction in marriage is a factor in predicting divorce. Steven L. Nock and Bradford Wilcox's, recent study, "What's Love Got To Do With It?: Equality, Equity, Commitment and Wom-

---

[49] Religious Coalition for Marriage, *A Letter from America's Religious Leaders in Defense of Marriage* (2006), available at http://www.religiouscoalitionformarriage.org.

[50] *See* data below.

en's Marital Quality,"[51] finds further that married women are happier if they hold traditional rather than egalitarian expectations about marriage, and if they share with their husbands high levels of church attendance and normative commitment to marriage as an institution. The study suggests that traditional wives may be happier because they expect less, and thus, when they get less, they are not disappointed.[52] At the same time, by expecting less, they might actually persuade their husbands to be more emotionally responsive and to invest more, because the husbands experience less conflict with their wives over the household division of labor.[53] In short, socialization for commitment and acceptance of traditional gender roles may be necessary to promote marital success.

Whether or not these positions are empirically true,[54] they represent fundamentally different approaches to family regulation. One emphasizes the internalization of norms of sexual restraint, a gendered division of family responsibilities, and commitment to marriage. The other insists on commitment to gender equality, financial and emotional preparation for childrearing, greater investment in women and children, and individual autonomy rather than community centered support for families. Fully implemented they support radically different lifestyles and family law systems.

2.2 Demographic Divisions

The debate over family values is intense not just because

---

[51] 84 *Social Forces* 1321(2006).

[52] *Id.* at 1324.

[53] *Id.* at 1325-28.

[54] For a response to Nock and Wilcox, for example, see Joanna Grossman And Linda McClain, "'Desperate Feminist Wives': Does The Quest For Marital Equality Doom Marital Happiness?" *Findlaw: Legal News And Commentary* (April 4, 2006), available at http://Writ.News.Findlaw. Com/Commentary/ 20060404_McClain.Html.

the positions differ ideologically, but because they correspond to different lived experiences, and different family systems in various parts of the country. Naomi Cahn and I are in the process of bringing together a variety of statistical measures that create a picture of these two different family systems. The statistics below provide a preliminary, broad-brush depiction of the differences in lifestyles that have emerged between the two systems.[55]

Take first the experience of marriage and childbearing. In 2000, the mean age of the mother at her first live birth for the nation as a whole was 24.9. Yet, the states with the highest average ages were entirely "blue:"[56] Massachusetts led (27.8), followed by Connecticut (27.2), New Jersey (27.1), New Hampshire (26.7), and New York (26.4). The states with the lowest average ages were entirely red: Arkansas had the lowest (22.7), followed by Louisiana and New Mexico (23.0), Oklahoma (23.1), and Wyoming (23.2).[57] Over the past 30 years, all states have experienced an increase in the mean age of mothers at which the first child is born, but the changes range from a 5.3 year increase in Massachusetts to a 1.9 year increase in Utah.[58]

Add in now the average age of marriage. In the United States, the median age of marriage for women is 25.1 and 26.7

---

[55] The data on age a demographics presented in this section will be published in greater detail in a forthcoming article by J. Carbone and N. Cahn, "Red Families v. Blue Families: Fedaralism in an Era of Polarization" (manuscript on file with the author). The single biggest limitation in these general statistics are the failure to break down the characteristics by race.

[56] The blue states are: California, Connecticut, Delaware, Hawaii, Illinois, Maine, Maryland, Massachusetts, Michigan, Minnesota, New Hampshire, New Jersey, New York, Oregon, Pennsylvania, Rhode Island, Vermont, Washington, and WIsconsin. The other 31 states are classified as red. *See* Michael Gastner, Cosma Shalizi,& Mark Newman, Maps and Cartograms of the 2004 US Presidential Election Results, available at http://www-personal.umich.edu/~mejn/election. As they emphasize, however, using a scale of percentage of voters results in a map that is more purple than red. *Id.; see* Robert J. Vanderbiel, *Election 2004 Results*, available at http://www.princeton.edu/~rvdb/JAVA/ election2004/

[57] T.J. Mathews & Brady E. Hamilton, "Mean Age of Mother, 1970-2000" 51 *Nat'l Vital Statistics Reports* 10,Table 3 (2002), available at http://www.cdc.gov/nchs/data/nvsr/nvsr51/nvsr51_01.pdf.

[58] *Id.*

for men.[59] In contrast, in 1960, the median age at first marriage was 20.3 for women and 22.8 for men.[60] The five states with the lowest median age of marriage for women are red: Utah (23.9, 21.9), Oklahoma (24.9, 22.7), Idaho (24.6, 22.8), Arkansas (25, 22.8), and Kentucky (25.3, 22.8). Correspondingly, the states with the highest median age of marriage for women are blue: Massachusetts (29.1, 27.4), New York (28.9, 27), Rhode Island (27.6, 26.7), Connecticut (28.9, 26.4), and New Jersey (28.6, 26.4).[61]

The differences between an average first birth at 22.7 years of age versus 27.8 years of age are substantial. So are the differences in marriage ages from 21.9 to 27.4 for women, and 23.9 to 29.1 for men. Testosterone levels peak in the mid-twenties. Helen Fisher observes that higher testosterone levels can reduce oxytocin and vasopressin, making attachment less likely,[62] and that "men with high baseline levels of testosterone marry less frequently, have more adulterous affairs, commit more spousal abuse, and divorce more often."[63] In addition, new research on brain development indicates that the areas in the brain associated with higher level reasoning, maturity and judgment do not fully mature until the mid-twenties. Less mature adults engage in higher levels of risk-taking, may have less impulse control, and display less judgment than they will at older ages. Couples marrying and giving birth in their late twenties should have fully developed mental faculties, and begun to settle down; couples still in

---

[59] Tallese Johnson &Jane Dye, "Indicators of Marriage and Fertility in the United States from the American Community Survey: 2000 to 2003," Table 1 (2005), available at http://www.census.gov/population/www/socdemo/fertility/mar-fert-slides.html.

[60] Infoplease, "Median Age at First marriage," available at http://www.infoplease.com/ipa/A0005061.html. On the other hand, in 1890, the median age of first marriage for men was 26.1, and 22.0 for women. *Id.*

[61] *See* http://www.census.gov/population/www/socdemo/fertility/slideshow/table01.csv.

[62] Helen Fisher, *Why We Love: The Nature and Chemistry of Romantic Love* (2004), at 90.

[63] *Id.*

their early twenties are still developing, experimenting, and "sowing their wild oats."

Divorce statistics bear out these predictions. The states with the highest divorce rates are red: Nevada, Wyoming, Arkansas, Kentucky, Mississippi, and Florida, while those with the lowest are primarily blue: Massachusetts, followed by Pennsylvania, North Dakota, Illinois, and Connecticut.[64] Researchers confirm that a younger age of marriage, lower economic status, and having a baby either prior to marriage or within the first seven months after marriage each increases the risk of divorce, holding other factors constant.[65]

These statistics suggest that red state characteristics combine the factors that make family instability more likely to occur. That is, younger marriages, especially if they are prompted by an improvident pregnancy, increase divorce rates. So, too, does lower socio-economic status, and red states may be more likely to reject middle class strategies because they are on average poorer (or on average poorer because they reject middle class family strategies).

The risk factors for red states involve more than divorce. Teen births are also higher. The five states with the lowest teen birth rates were New Hampshire, Vermont, Massachusetts, Connecticut, and Maine, while the states with the highest teen birth rates were Texas, New Mexico, Mississippi, Arizona, and Arkansas.[66] On the other hand, while the percent of nonmarital teen births in the United States was 82 percent in 2004, the states with the lowest percentage of teen births to nonmarital mothers were: Idaho, with 64 percent; Utah, with 66 percent; Texas, with 73 percent; and Colorado, Kentucky,

---

[64] U.S. Census Bureau, *Statistical Abstract of the United States 2005-2006*, at 93 (Table No. 117), available at http://www.census.gov/prod/2005pubs/06statab/vitstat.pdf.

[65] Barbara Dafoe Whitehead & David Popenoe, "The State of Our Unions: The Social Health of Marriage in America 2004" (2004), at Box 2, available at http://marriage.rutgers.edu/Publications/SOOU/TEXTSOOU2004.htm#Divorce

[66] Child Trends, "Teen Birth Rates Ranked Lowest to Highest, 2003 (Rates Per 1,000 Females Ages 15-19)," available at http://www.childtrends.org/Files/FAAG2006StatebyState.pdf.

and Wyoming, each with 74 percent.[67] Those states with the highest percentage of nonmarital teen births were Massachusetts (92 percent), Delaware, Pennsylvania, and Rhode Island (91 percent), and Connecticut and Maryland (90 percent).[68] In other words, one set of states has lower teen birth rates, and higher rates of nonmarital births, while a second set tends to have higher teen birth rates, but more births occurring within marriage,[69] and correspondingly younger ages of marriage.[70]

Abortion ratios complete the picture. Blue states led the ratios of abortions per 1,000 live births: New York, Delaware, Washington, Massachusetts, and Connecticut each had a ratio over 300. The states with the lowest abortion ratios were red: Colorado, Utah, Idaho, and South Dakota each had a ratio under 100.[71] Similarly, states with the lowest abortion rates – number of abortions per 1000 women between the ages of 15 to 44 – were Colorado, Utah, Idaho, Kentucky, and South Dakota, while those with the highest abortion rates were New

---

[67] ChildTrends, "Facts at a Glance" (2006), at Table 1, available at http://www.childtrends.org/Files/FAAG2006.pdf

[68] *Id.*

[69] Vermont, New Hampshire, and Maine, among the states with the lowest teen birth rate, also had high percentages of nonmarital teen births: in Vermont, the figure was 87%, New Hampshire (89%), and Maine (88%). *Id.* The percent of births to teen mothers with respect to all births in the state was highest in New Mexico (17%), followed by Mississippi (16%), Arkansas and Louisiana (15%), and Alabama and Oklahoma (14%). *Id.* The lowest percentages were in Massachusetts, New Hampshire, New Jersey, and Vermont (6%), along with Connecticut, Minnesota, New York, and Utah (7%). *Id.*

[70] The overall rate of non-marital births is harder to assess, in part, because of the influence of race. The states with the highest overall rates of non-marital births (Washington D.C., Mississippi, and Lousiana) all have high African-American populations. The states with the lowest rates (Utah, Idaho, and Minnesota) have much lower rates. *See* http://www.guttmacher.org/pubs/ib22.html.

[71] Laurie D. Elam-Evans, et al., "Abortion Surveillance- United States, 2000" (2003), at Table 3, available at http://www.cdc.gov/mmwr/preview/mmwrhtml/ss5212a1.htm. Florida and Louisiana had low rates as well, but did not report the number of abortions with respect to in-state residents. *Id.*

York, Delaware, Washington, New Jersey and Rhode Island.[72]

These figures confirm once again the existence of two different family systems: one creating pressures for early marriage and childbearing. The other for avoiding teen births and early marriages, through measures that include a greater resort to abortion.

The final figures involve overall fertility. The percent of childless women is highest in the Northeast states, and lowest in the southern states.[73] The nineteen states with the highest fertility rates are red, while the 16 states with the lowest fertility rates are blue.[74] In the United States, there are 1,182 children born for every 1,000 women.[75] Alaska has the highest fertility rate, with 1,435 children born per 1,000 women, followed by Arkansas (1,418), Utah and Mississippi (1,393), and South Dakota (1,368). The states with the lowest fertility rates are: Maryland (991), Vermont (1,000), Massachusetts (1,020), Maine (1,022), and Delaware (1,023).

While these statistics cannot provide a complete view of different cultural values, they suggest that red state and blue state families are living different lives.

---

[72] *Id.* States with incomplete measures were again excluded, as was Washington D.C..

[73] Jane Lawler Dye, "Fertility of American Women: June 2004" (2005), at 4, Table 2, available at http://www.census.gov/prod/2005pubs/p20-555.pdf. The percentage of childless women was 48% in the northeast, which includes Maine, New Hampshire, Vermont, Massachusetts, Rhode Island, Connecticut, New York, New Jersey, and Pennsylvania and 42.5% in the south, which included Delaware, Maryland, DC, Virginia, West Virgina, North Carolina, South Carolina, Georgia, Florida, Kentucky, Tennessee, Alabama, Mississippi, Arkansas, Louisiana, Oklahoma, and Texas. The statistics did not include a further breakdown by state.

[74] Steve Sailer, "Birth Gap: How birthrates color the Electoral Map, The American Conservative" (2004), available at http://www.amconmag.com/2004_12_06/cover.html.

[75] U.S. Census Bureau, "Fertility of American Women" (2004), at Table S1, available at http://www.census.gov/population/socdemo/fertility/tabS1.xls. Washington D.C. is, once again, an outlier, with a fertility rate of 776. States with the lowest fertility rates for never-married women were mixed, with Utah, a red state, with the lowest rate of 208, followed by Delaware (213), Minnesota (234), North Dakota (241), Idaho (247), and New Hampshire (254). *Id.*

2.3 Legal Fractures

The largest difference in the two family systems involves the regulation of sexuality. One system deregulates sexuality, but discourages early childbearing; the other system attempts to reinforce the link between sexuality and marriage. Comprehensive differences, some minor, others profound, divide the family law systems among the states. Two flashpoints, in particular though, symbolize the divide among the states.

The first is abortion. Given the Supreme Court's recognition of a women's right to choose, a central battleground has been parental notification laws.[76] Carol Sanger argues that, although these laws are framed as representing children's interests, they in fact represent a political decision on behalf of third parties to prevent minors from obtaining abortions, to reinforce parental authority, and to punish the girls for their sexual behavior.[77] Childbirth as the price of illicit sex is an important factor in reinforcing a traditional understanding of sexual morality.[78]

An overwhelming majority of states require some form of parental involvement, generally subject to the judicial bypass option. In 21 states, parental consent is required before a minor can obtain an abortion, with two red states (Missis-

---

[76] *See Ayotte v. Planned Parenthood*, U.S., 126 S. Ct. 961, 966, n.1 (2006) (noting that 44 states have enacted laws mandating parental involvement. In four of those states, there is no exception to the parental involvement requirement based on an emergency concerning the minor's health).

[77] Carol Sanger, "Regulating Teenage Abortion in the United States: Politics and Policy," 18 *Intl. J. L., Pol'y & Fam.* 305 (2004), at 315.

[78] The argument extends to more than abortion. *See, e.g.,* Russell Shorto, "Contra-Contraception," *N.Y. Times Mag.* (May 7, 2007) ("'We see a direct connection between the practice of contraception and the practice of abortion,' says Judie Brown, president of the American Life League, an organization that has battled abortion for 27 years but that, like others, now has a larger mission. 'The mind-set that invites a couple to use contraception is an antichild mind-set,' she told me. 'So when a baby is conceived accidentally, the couple already have this negative attitude toward the child. Therefore seeking an abortion is a natural outcome. We oppose all forms of contraception.'").

sippi and North Dakota) mandating that both parents consent, while in 13 states, parental notification is required.[79] In another nine states – Alaska, California, Idaho, Illinois, Montana, Nevada, New Hampshire, New Jersey, and New Mexico - enforcement of statutes requiring parental involvement have been permanently enjoined.[80] Seven states, all of which are blue – Connecticut, Hawaii, Maine, New York, Oregon, Vermont, and Washington – do not require any form of parental involvement in minors' abortion decisions.[81] Studies show that parental involvement laws result in fewer abortions and more births.[82]

The second and most perplexing issue is gay marriage. Supporters of the new middle class model adopted by Blue America simply do not get it. One op-ed piece titled "Gay Marriage: Why Would It Affect Me?" observed:

> When opponents talk about the "defense of marriage," they lose me. James Dobson's Focus on the Family just sent out a mailer to 2.5 million homes saying: "The homosexual activists' movement is poised to administer a devastating and potentially fatal blow to the traditional family." And I say, "Huh?" How does anyone's pledge of love and commitment turn into a

---

[79] Guttmacher Institute, "State Policies in Brief: Parental Involvement in Minors' Abortions" (Jan. 1, 2006), available at http://www.guttmacher.org/statecenter/spibs/spib_PIMA.pdf.

[80] *Id.*

[81] *Id.*

[82] *See, e.g.,* Michael J. New, "Using Natural Experiments to Analyze the Impact of State Legislation on the Incidence of Abortion" (2006), available at www.heritage.org/Researc/Family/cda06-01.cfm (finding: when a parental involvement law is enacted, the abortion rate decreases by 16.37 abortions for every thousand live births [the abortion ratio] and the abortion rate decrease by 1.15 abortions for every thousand women between the ages of 15 to 44 [the abortion rate]. Parental involvement laws that are passed and then nullified by the judiciary result in modest increases in the abortion rate and a modest decline in the abortion ratio). *See also* Theodore Joyce, Robert Kaestner, & Silvie Colman, "Changes in Abortions and Births and the Texas Parental Notification Law," 354 *New Eng. L. Med.* 1031 (2006).

fatal blow to families?[83]

Dobson responded, referring to Genesis:

> The legalization of homosexual marriage will quickly destroy the traditional family... [W]hen the State sanctions homosexual relationships and gives them its blessing, the younger generation becomes confused about sexual identity and quickly loses its understanding of lifelong commitments, emotional bonding, sexual purity, the role of children in a family, and from a spiritual perspective, the "sanctity" of marriage. Marriage is reduced to something of a partnership that provides attractive benefits and sexual convenience, but cannot offer the intimacy described in Genesis. Cohabitation and short-term relationships are the inevitable result.[84]

This debate replicates the earlier disagreements on the regulation of morality that occupied Hart and Devlin. Naomi Cahn and I have argued that the biological evidence suggests that human beings as a species are in fact more geared to serial monogamy (*i.e.*, "cohabitation and short-term relationships") than long-term fidelity.[85] The more difficult it is to rechannel behavior, the more important (and fragile) internalized norms become. Ariela Dubler writes that the Christian constructions of sexual morality that influenced American judges and continue to influence contemporary politics "posited marriage as the site where lust was

---

[83] Dr. James Dobson, "Eleven Arguments Against Same-Sex Marriage" (May 23, 2004), available at http://www.family.org/cforum/extras/a0032427.cfm (quoting Steve Blow, "Gay Marriage: Why Would it Affect Me?" *Dallas Morning News*).

[84] *Id.*

[85] June Carbone & Naomi Cahn, "The Biological Basis of Commitment: Does One Size Fit All?," 25 *Women's Rights L. Rep.* 223 (2004).

transformed into virtue."[86] If it is part of human nature to experience lust, to be tempted to engage in illicit acts that range from bestiality to adultery, then the preservation of marriage as a privileged state is necessary to resist those temptations. Redefining marriage to include "sinful acts"[87] or to recognize relationships based on something other than the unity of sex, reproduction, and childrearing undermines the enterprise. If anyone can claim the blessings of marriage, what is the point of abstinence? If the relationship does not elevate those within it, why work to maintain the institution when life turns difficult? The issue is inflamed further by the identification of gays and sometimes lesbians with greater promiscuity, within or without marriage.[88] Yet, for the upwardly mobile middle class, who replaced abstinence with an emphasis on emotional and financial preparation for childrearing, the argument is barely cognizable. The "huh?" response is real.

State legislation reflects the divide. Thirty-three states now have statutory bans on marriage for same-sex couples, and

---

[86] Ariela R. Dubler, "Immoral Purposes: Marriage and the Genus of Illicit Sex," 115 *Yale L.J.* 756 (2006), at 763.

[87] *See Id.* at 812 (commenting: "Marriage is at once powerful to confer legal privileges and to shield people from the dangers of sexual illicitness, and powerless to protect itself from the taint of those very illicit practices.").

[88] *See, e.g.,* Religious Coalition for Marriage, "Top 10 Social Scientific Arguments Against Same Sex Marriage," available at http://www.religiouscoalitionformarriage.org/html/top_ten.php, observing that:

> In the first edition of his book in defense of marriage, Virtually Normal, Andrew Sullivan wrote: "There is more likely to be greater understanding of the need for extramarital outlets between two men than between a man and a woman." One recent study of civil unions and marriages in Vermont suggests this is a very real concern. More than 79 percent of heterosexual married men and women, along with lesbians in civil unions, reported that they strongly valued sexual fidelity. Only about 50 percent of gay men in civil unions valued sexual fidelity.

In addition, younger ages of marriage also change the context for recognizing homosexuality, with gays and lesbians more likely to "come out of the closet" in Red America at the time of divorce, linking homosexuality in the minds of some with adultery. In communities with later average ages at marriage, and more gay friendly environments, the link does not exist.

seven have enacted constitutional amendments banning gay marriage.[89] Sixteen of the seventeen states with some form of constitutional amendment or statute adopting broader anti-gay measures are red, while only one is blue (Michigan). The only red states not to have some form of anti-gay measure are Wyoming and New Mexico. In contrast, the other seven states without any form of anti-gay measure are Maryland, Massachusetts, New Jersey, New York, Connecticut, Rhode Island, and Vermont – lean blue. The six states to extend same-sex couples legal recognition and benefits comparable to marriage are all blue.[90]

Efforts to control sexuality extend across a broad range of issues. They include greater scrutiny into non-marital cohabitation in custody cases, continuing recognition of adultery in custody or financial awards, and the more celebrated efforts to adopt covenant marriage. While adoption of such measures is far from uniform, enforcement may be uneven, and support for the return of fault in divorce actions is mixed even in the reddest of red states. These measures, together with the high profile fights over abortion and gay marriage, suggest the existence of two internally coherent, but incompatible family law systems.

---

[89] *See* http://www.thetaskforce.org/downloads/MarriageMap_06.pdf

[90] *See* Leslie Harris, "Same-Sex Unions Around the World: Marriage, Civil Unions, Registered Partnerships—What are the Differences and Why do they Matter?," 19 *Probate & Property* 31 (September/October 2005), at 33; Human Rights Campaign, "Relationship Recognition in the U.S.," available at http://www.hrc.org/Template.cfm?Section=Center&CONTENTID=2 6860&TEMPLATE=/ContentManagement/ContentDisplay.cfm. Maine's legislation, which is the most limited, allows both same-sex and opposite sex couples to register for domestic partnership, a status which grants various rights in protective proceedings and intestacy; California, Connecticut, and Vermont offer couples almost all of the rights associated with marriage (Vermont and Connecticut's legislation are limited to same-sex partners); New Jersey and Hawaii offer somewhat less expansive rights. Human Rights Campaign, "Relationship Recognition in the U.S.," available at http://www.hrc.org/Template.cfm?Section=Center&CO NTENTID=26860&TEMPLATE=/ContentManagement/ContentDisplay.cfm.

3. CAN INDIVIDUALS EXERCISE AUTONOMY IN THE
SELECTION OF INSTITUTIONS?

The emerging differences in family law raise an issue that does not exist at a time of consensus about family values: *viz.*, how much deference should be given, in the selection of institutions as opposed to private beliefs and practices, to individual autonomy. The question is one with deep roots within liberal democracies.

John Rawls, after his enormously influential theory of justice,[91] wrote *Political Liberalism* precisely to address the obligations of liberalism in such circumstances. He observed that a "modern democratic society is characterized not simply by a pluralism of comprehensive religious, philosophical, and moral doctrines but by a pluralism of incompatible yet reasonable comprehensive doctrines."[92] To deal with this plurality of views, Rawls advanced the idea of the "overlapping consensus," which he defined not just as a modus vivendi to which parties agreed to the extent that it advances their short term self-interest, but rather as a rule they accept because it reflects a deep moral commitment supported by their individual comprehensive schemes.[93] Rawls emphasized that the "fact that people affirm the same political conception on those grounds does not make their affirming it any less religious, philosophical, or moral, as the case may be, since the grounds sincerely held determine the nature of their affirmation."[94]

Opposition to polygamy at the time of the nineteenth century cases – and probably still today – provides such an example. The United States in the nineteenth century thought of itself

---

[91] John Rawls, *A Theory of Justice* (1971).

[92] John Rawls, *Political Liberalism* (1993), at xvi.

[93] *Id.* at 147.

[94] *Id.* at 147-48.

as a Christian nation, if not a Baptist, or Catholic one, and all of the different Christian churches, and most modern secular and moral philosophies in the United States today, oppose polygamy. Accordingly, the U.S. as a liberal state could justify outlawing polygamy without necessarily embracing all or any one of the different justifications for doing so. Moreover, as the Supreme Court's invocation of Lieber's political philosophy indicated, the Court could uphold such a restriction not just because of widespread consensus, but because it found such principles consistent with equality and equal respect within a liberal democracy.[95]

Conversely, in dealing with churches, Rawls, the U.S. Constitution, and almost all theories of liberalism distinguish between the authority churches hold over their members because of the members' consent, and the authority of the state to compel membership, or to enforce the precepts of a particular church or religion.[96] Liberalism began as a response to the wars fought over established churches,[97] and neutrality among competing visions of the good may be its most important contribution. The American state may thus permit free expression and encourage religious worship as critical to the inculcation of virtue,[98] but still stay out of regulation of churches as institutions. Indeed, the Universal Life Church, which offers on-line ordination to anyone who applies, provides a wonderful example.[99] The state does not oversee the church or its power to grant ordination. But it does recognize the ordination as conferring the power to conduct a marriage ceremony.

---

[95] *Id.* at 337-38.

[96] *Id.* at 221-222.

[97] *Id.* at xxiv.

[98] William A. Galston, *Liberal Purposes; Goods, Virtue, and Diversity in the Liberal State* (1991), at 257.

[99] *See* http://www.ulc.org.

Individual states could, of course, deal with the clash in family systems on the same model as religion, and some countries have. Commentators have proposed that the state recognize only civil unions; that is, the state administer only the financial and practical consequences of marriage. Ceremonial marriage along with its ritual and emotional components would be relegated to the private sphere. The state would replace marriage licenses with civil union certificates allowing couples to choose the church, synagogue, commitment ceremony, or universal life minister of their choice to perform the ceremony – or to restrict their relationship to the civil aspects recognized by the state.[100]

This approach, however, would institutionalize the blue state deregulation of sexuality more than it would maintain parity among the competing systems. The problem is that formal neutrality, desirable though it may be with respect to speech and private conduct, and critical though it may be with respect to such essential clashes as those over religion, may not be enough to address the expressive role of the state. Libertarian Robert Nozick has written that:

> [w]ithin the operations of democratic institutions, too, we want expressions of the values that concern us and bind us together. The libertarian position I once propounded now seems to me seriously inadequate, in part because it did not fully knit the humane considerations and joint cooperative activities it left room for more closely into its fabric. It neglected the symbolic importance of an official political concern with issues or problems, as a way of marking their importance or urgency, and hence of expressing, intensifying, channeling, encouraging, and validating

[100] Edward A. Zelinsky, "Symposium Abolishing Civil Marriage: Deregulating Marriage: The Pro-Marriage Case for Abolishing Civil Marriage," 27 *Cardozo L. Rev.* 1161 (2006).

our private actions and concerns toward them.[101]

The expression of traditional family values in red states, and for many in the country as a whole, is a matter of urgency because of the state of our families. Channeling appropriate intimate behavior is challenging, and the institutions that have historically inculcated and policed family norms have atrophied. The problems are particularly great for those ready to assume adult responsibilities at younger ages, and for those most directly threatened by the transition to a post-industrial economy. The reaffirmation of shared values and the "symbolic importance of... official political concern" becomes particularly important when those values are seen as under assault.

The ability of the state to act at all in this arena, therefore, involves a choice between the two sets of values, and it is not a choice that can be avoided: doing nothing reaffirms the traditional state sanction of heterosexual marriage consistent with the promotion of traditional notions of sexual morality, and deregulating marriage in favor of civil unions or private ceremonies affirms equality and choice at the expense of traditional family values.[102]

Nozick suggests, consistent with his celebration of liberty, that the solution is not to avoid all expression of controversial values, but rather "when someone conscientiously objects on moral grounds to the *goals* of a public policy," he or she should be allowed to opt out of that policy to the extent possible.[103] He emphasizes, however, that while some even "propose removing anything morally controversial from the political realm, leaving it for private endeavor..., this would prevent the majority from jointly and publicly affirming its

---

[101] Robert Nozick, *The Examined Life* (1989), at 286-87.

[102] Though not, as we have argued above, the family values of financial regularity and commitment to children.

[103] *Id.* at 290. (Emphasis in original).

values."[104] Instead, he advocates balancing the symbolic expression of the majority against the individual's ability to resist compelled participation.

I believe, despite my preference for blue state values, that Nozick is right that the state should retain the power to express the values of the majority,[105] and that within the American family law context that means preserving some space for the expression of different values in different states.[106] States can choose which values to promote on a majoritarian basis, and provide for their symbolic promotion, and active inculcation through education and voluntary programs.[107] I believe that the limits on state power and the preservation of autonomy lie in avoiding (where possible) a "symbolic affront" in the clash of values, and preserving the autonomy of individuals to express different beliefs, and participate in private consensual conduct at odds with public norms.[108]

---

[104] *Id.*

[105] This argument depends, however, on representation in the expression of values. It is one thing for a legislature representing majoritarian views to promote values that affect all citizens equally. (Legislative efforts to stigmatize adultery, for example, carry greater moral weight when unfaithful legislators are among those affected). It is another thing, however, when the majority exercises political power to stigmatize behavior primarily associated with a minority. It is arguable, for example, that welfare reform involved imposition of the views of a majority (marriage promoting middle class whites) through regulation of a program disproportionately affecting a minority (welfare recipients who are disproportionately poor people of color) who might embrace different values or priorities. To that end, promotion of the unity of sex, marriage, and procreation by a heterosexual majority might be legitimate, but prohibition of same-sex (but not different-sex) sodomy clearly would not be.

[106] See Libby S. Adler, "Federalism and Family," 8 *Colum. J. Gender & L.* 197 (1999), at 197-99 ("Under our federalist system, the axiom has it, family law resides within the province of the states.... As a factual matter, however, the federal government exerts tremendous power over family.").

[107] Individual students or families, however, should have the option of not participating in public education to which they object. The ability not to participate in sex education classes or discussions of controversial literature provide existing examples.

[108] This leaves open the question of what behavior, such as polygamy, can still be banned as inconsistent with the overlapping consensus or the harm principle discussed above. *See* William N. Eskridge, Jr., "Body Politics: *Lawrence v. Texas* and the Constitution of Disgust and

The idea of "symbolic affront" requires explication. All choices of one set of values over another involve a "symbolic affront" to those rejected. Indeed, state inculcation of shared values necessarily involves efforts to undermine opposing views. Nonetheless, clashes between values do not always involve polar opposites. For example, those who would affirm women's equality and autonomy, and maintain that a woman's most important obligation to her children involves deferring childbearing until she is able to optimally provide for the children she rears, do not necessarily advocate abortion as an unqualified right. Instead, they see it as instrumental to values they do hold. Where different states vary in the choice of primary values, and both value choices are defensible, national decisions and the resolution of interstate conflicts should attempt to minimize the symbolic affront to values actively promoted in some states, but not in others.[109] In the abortion context, for example, this may mean that public funding, to the extent it occurs at all, exists at the state level, where it can be implemented in a way that complements the expression of shared values, rather than the federal

---

Contagion," 57 *Fla. L. Rev.* 1011 (2005), at 1056, observing that:

> The original principles undergirding the Fourteenth Amendment plus the admonition against raising the stakes of politics can be synthesized into doctrinal variables - features of a liberty - infringing policy that render it more or less constitutionally vulnerable under the Fourteenth Amendment. So a morals law that criminalizes conduct that (1) is no longer widely criminalized and (2) does not seem to impose harm on third parties but (3) is important to a coherent and well-organized social group is most constitutionally objectionable. Like consensual sodomy, fornication easily fits within this unregulable core: Most states have decriminalized it, there is virtually no evidence of third-party harms, and a whole generation (the baby boomers) consider the right to fornicate important to their lives, or formative experiences in their youths.

[109] This provides a basis for distinguishing *Loving v. Virginia*, 388 U.S. 1 (1967). By the time the case was decided in 1967, the moral basis of the anti-miscegenation statutes, which rested on an ideal of racial purity, could be said to be in disrepute, whatever the majority response in some state polls might have been. The Court accordingly held that the Virginia statute served no legitimate purpose. *Loving* 388 U.S. at 11-12. The identification of marriage with the unity of sex, procreation, and childrearing, while under assault, cannot at this point be said to be in disrepute. *See* discussion *infra*.

level.

With respect to the expression of individual views and conduct, Nozick provides the example of a conscientious objector, who he argues should be permitted to substitute those taxes allocated for war for contributions of equal or greater value to another government program, and his suggestion works in the blue states. That is, someone who objects to state contributions to family planning or abortion services might be given the option of redirecting tax dollars. Indeed, the federal government has largely eliminated federal funding for abortion and similar services for reasons akin to those Nozick advances.

The larger issues, however, involve the autonomy of individuals to order their lives, their relationships, and their families. No state is likely to compel participation in marriage, and though the shot-gun marriage may still be alive in some parts of the country (and still apparently desired in Congress), direct coercion is rare.[110] Instead, the difficulty arises most from the symbolic affront that occurs from placing the imprimatur of the state on – or actively condemning – controversial relationships.

To the extent that opponents of same-sex marriage have a legitimate basis on which to invoke the power of the state on a majoritarian basis, it comes from the identification of marriage, on a historical, emotional, and religious level, with procreation, and the dissonance that arises from extending that relationship to non-procreative unions.[111] Conversely,

---

[110] It is sadly more of an issue with respect to parental notification statutes; these issues, however, turn on the relationship of parental authority over a minor. *See* Sanger, supra note 77.

[111] *See, e.g.,* Chai Feldblum's summary of the arguments, observing that "[d]uring early congressional debates on marriage, opponents of marriage equality contended that marriage for same-sex couples would result in condoning gay sexual coupling and would thereby radically redefine and irrevocably shatter the moral foundations of both marriage and society. In later congressional debates, opponents shifted their argument to the claim that having a "mom and a dad" represented the optimal environment for passing on moral and social values to children." Chai R. Feldblum, "Symposium: Gay Is Good: The Moral Case for Marriage Equality and More," 17 *Yale J.L. & Feminism* 139 (2005), at 141.

the strongest claim to state recognition of same-sex marriage involves what Justice Scalia has referred to as the "homosexual agenda," "directed at eliminating the moral opprobrium that has traditionally attached to homosexual conduct."[112] Affirmation of same-sex marriage involves practical and symbolic affirmation of the values of autonomy, equality and fairness.[113] It also involves recognition of the parenting status of two adults who may have undertaken important roles in children's lives.

Those states, therefore, that wish to affirm equality and responsibility to children while deregulating sexuality, should encourage the creation of private spaces for the expression of traditional values. The separation of civil and religious marriage provides a perfect example.

For those states that wish to affirm the continuing limitation of marriage to a man and a woman, the answer may be to distinguish the symbolic affirmation of values from practical compulsion, and to separate federal recognition of basic rights governing conduct from greater state autonomy to express values.

The first component in this balance is national protection for private conduct. Ariela Dubler argues that Kennedy's opinion in *Lawrence* represents the ultimate dismantling of marriage as the bright line between licit and illicit sex.[114] *Lawrence* instead effectively recognizes three categories of intimate behavior: state-sanctioned activity within marriage, illicit sex that continues to be criminalized such as prostitution or polygamy, and a new category that is neither approved nor condemned. Kennedy takes pains in *Lawrence* to

---

[112] *Lawrence*, 539 U.S. at 602.

[113] Feldblum, *supra* note 111, at 144.

[114] Dubler, *supra* note 86, at 812. *See*, however, Roderick Hills' description of *Lawrence* as constitutionalizing the consensus of the states on the deregulation of consensual sodomy. Roderick M. Hills, Jr., *The Individual Right to Federalism in the Rehnquist Court* (manuscript on file with author).

recognize the potential value of same-sex bonds, but he deliberately stops short of insisting that the state must extend formal recognition to the relationships. In doing so, he creates a protected space for individual behavior while minimizing the symbolic affront to majoritarian values.

Second, the harm principle should limit the policing of other aspects of traditional morality as it relates to children. Virtually all custody precedents, for example, require a nexus between sexual behavior and children's interests as a consideration in custody cases.[115] Such cases allow symbolic reinforcement of traditional values without (*if* effectively followed) too great an infringement on private conduct.

Third, while interstate recognition of same-sex unions may trigger resistance, adoptions and property judgments should clearly come under the protection of the full faith and credit clause. These court orders may not necessarily involve state embrace of the underlying adult unions; yet, they are of enormous potential significance in the private ordering of individual lives.[116]

The abortion cases pose greater challenges, in part, because the issue involves not just a clash over family values, but deep, religiously based divisions over the definition of life. I believe that at least part of the reason for the enduring clash over abortion is the fact that the Supreme Court's decision in *Roe v. Wade*[117] does pose a symbolic affront to deeply held values that has not dissipated with the passage of time.

---

[115] *See* Leslie J. Harris, Lee E. Teitelbaum, & June Carbone, *Family Law* (2005), at 666.

[116] The traditional rule that states must recognize out of state marriages unless the marriages offend the basic public policy of the states, in contrast with the full faith and credit clause, does not require deference to the different values of different jurisdictions. Instead, the home state is free to choose to affirm its values at the expense of a sister state's. Because of this legal framework, the symbolic meaning of recognition of an out of state marriage is greater than the symbolic meaning of an out of state adoption or property judgment. *See* June Carbone, "Assisted Reproduction in an Era of Polarization: An Institutional Examination of Why Adoption May Be the New Battleground for the Recognition of Partnership," *Capital L. Rev.* (forthcoming) (2006).

[117] 410 U.S. 113 (1973).

I will leave the definitions of life to others, but argue that the approach I have maintained with respect to same-sex marriage also holds with respect to abortion in at least two respects.

First, parental notification measures involve a symbolic reaffirmation of parental authority over sexual conduct. Protection for vulnerable minors should come through safeguards built into implementation of the procedures rather than a direct assault on the principle.

Second, greater protection should be accorded to interstate travel. Choice may be meaningless without access.

Finally, as noted above, the ability of individuals to opt out, or express disapproval should be respected. As a practical matter, this involves a balance between securing access to abortion and family planning services and allowing individual providers of medical services not to participate in actions they find objectionable.[118]

4. CONCLUSION

Both Kennedy's *Lawrence* majority opinion and Scalia's dissent recognized that the expression of values reflects evolving, rather than static norms. They disagreed on the respective roles of the legislature and the courts in recognizing changes over time. The argument in this paper suggests that the evolution also reflects, not just geographic divisions, but differing responses to class, gender, and economic shifts that may play out at different times and with different consequences in various parts of the country. In the face of such fundamental differences, choosing one set of values over another may simply deepen a polarization that encourages not just the rejection, but also the disrespect of opposing

---

[118] This clearly means that an individual doctor should not be compelled to perform an abortion. It does not mean, however, that the state may not guarantee access to abortion services by requiring that all doctors employed in certain clinics be willing to provide abortion services as a condition of employment.

views and those who hold them. This paper has argued that a
liberal democracy ought to be able to promote controversial
values, but it should do so in ways that minimize "the symbolic affront" to minority perspectives and preserve the individual autonomy of expression and conduct that leaves room for
institutional evolution.

In the meantime, this solution insists on recognition of
differing roles for legislatures and those courts that would
impose uniform national results as a matter of constitutional right. The articulation of majoritarian values can be an
appropriate role for the legislature even in the face of a
vigorous dissent. The courts, in contrast, should protect
individual autonomy in the expression of beliefs, participation
in symbolic activities, and private conduct. Bill Eskridge, who
has strongly advocated recognition of same-sex marriage in
other contexts, maintains that:

> The politics of tolerance strongly counsels that the
> Court do nothing for the time being. Either rejecting
> or endorsing the constitutionality of same-sex marriage
> bars would immediately raise the stakes of national
> politics. The reason is that the issue of same-sex
> marriage not only remains divisive, but also divides in
> ways that cut to the core of people's identities. Under
> these circumstances, the Court's best strategy is to
> leave the matter to the states, the famous "laboratories
> for experimentation."[119]

It is important to emphasize that allowing room for state
promotion of controversial values holds only so long as the
expression of values represents defensible values important
to legitimate state interests, and the states, through the
legislature or the courts, protect what might otherwise be
unpopular groups from oppression. At the point where it can

---

[119] Eskridge, *supra* note 108, at 1057-58.

no longer be said that any legitimate state interest is served, or where majoritarian values have so shifted to undermine the basis for the values expressed, the balance between symbolic expression and individual autonomy may change. Thus, *Loving v. Virginia*,[120] which in many ways involved the same type of clash between a traditional vision of the role of marriage and a claim of equal rights for an oppressed majority, avoided the type of symbolic affront described here, because the anti-miscegenation principle enshrined in the challenged statute had lost its legitimacy. While in some parts of the country the case against same-sex marriage is equally tenuous and may some day be in the nation as a whole, in other places the continuing celebration of the unity of marriage, sex, and procreation retains enough integrity to counsel deference to majoritarian expression. Autonomy in the definition of family, as a state created status, thus remains unattainable.

---

[120] 388 U.S. 1 (1967).

Approaches to Autonomy in Capital Punishment and Assisted Suicide

Kandis Scott

Literature tells us that death is not the worst we can suffer and that personal autonomy may often be just as important as the preservation of life itself. In Euripides's *Hecuba*, Polyxena refuses imprisonment, preferring to die nobly. The father in *The Reader*,[1] tells his law student son there is no justification for superseding others' views of what is good for them, even if they will become unhappy about their choices later, because "we're not talking about happiness, we're talking about dignity and freedom." Even on a popular American TV program, such as *Law and Order* the writers find it plausible that a defendant should acknowledge criminal responsibility and elect to die, as an expression of contrition and free will.[2] Dramatists represent and even glorify those who choose death, but it is legislatures, courts, and defense lawyers who sometimes control the decision in practice. What duties should a lawyer and the justice system have in those rare cases when a person sentenced to death seeks prompt execution?

Twelve percent of the 477 persons executed between 1977 and 1997 were "death volunteers:" they chose death without exhausting all their possible appeals.[3] This growing

---

[1] Bernhard Schlink, *The Reader* (New York: Pantheon Books, 1995). I thank my research assistant, Charlene Powell, for her substantial contributions to this essay.

[2] *Law & Order: Bad Girl* (NBC television broadcast, 29 April 1998).

[3] Ann W. O'Neill, "When Prisoners Have a Death Wish: A Rising Number of Inmates are Volunteering to be Executed. For some in the Grips of Depression, it is a Desperate Bid to Gain

phenomenon[4] presents a conflict between the autonomy of a criminal sentenced to death and society's interest in just execution. The European and American death-with-dignity laws offer guidance in answering whether we should honor the request of an inmate awaiting execution.

1. CAPITAL PUNISHMENT PROCESS

Some basic features of "capital prosecutions," prosecution of crimes punishable by death, are the same in all United States' jurisdictions. After a guilty verdict is entered, the court conducts an adversarial hearing before a jury on the issue of punishment. The defendant may argue for life imprisonment, rather than execution, at this sentencing hearing.[5] If the result is a sentence of death, the defendant is permitted appeals and other procedures to challenge the conviction, the sentence, or both.[6] In 37 of the 38 states permitting capital punishment, there is automatic judicial review of every death sentence.[7]

Control Over Their Lives" *L.A. Times*, 11 Sept. 1998, at A1.

[4] Between 1976, when capital punishment was reinstated, and 2001, 10% of execution were voluntary. Robert Anthony Phillips, "The Rush to the Death Chamber," *Christian Science Monitor*, 11 May 2001, at USA1. Sixty of the ninety volunteers were executed in the six years between 1995-2001. *Id.*

[5] *See Gregg v. Georgia*, 428 U.S. 153 (1976) (approving Georgia's death penalty statute, which provided for bifurcated trial).

[6] I use the terms "appeals" or "challenges" to refer to any post-trial procedure intended to seek freedom or to mitigate the sentence of the defendant, including collateral challenges, such as: requesting habeas corpus, appeals in both federal and state courts of the conviction and sentence, and clemency requests.

The number of possible appeals has been limited by the Antiterrorism and Effective Death Penalty Act of 1996 (AEDPA). Ronn Gehring, Note, *"Tyler v. Cain:*A Fork in the Path for Habeas Corpus or the End of the Road for Collateral Review?"* 36 *Akron L.Rev.* 181, 192, 200-01 (2002). AEDPA "eliminated a reviewing court's discretion to determine if it should hear a second or successive habeas petition by mandating the dismissal of second or successive petitions" where the petition does not present a new claim. *Id.* Additionally, the Act gives both state and federal inmates one year from the date of the final judgment in which to file a petition. *Id.*

[7] Julie Levinsohn Miller, Note: "Dignity or Death Row: Are Death Row Rights to Die Diminished? A Comparison of the Right to Die for the Terminally Ill and the Terminally

This is often a very lengthy process due to the difficulties in finding volunteer attorneys for convicted defendants.[8] The defendant also has the choice of filing discretionary appeals and other challenges, such as habeas corpus petitions.[9] Prisoners who file all possible appeals remain on death row an average of 11 to 20 years,[10] because the appellate process is slow, and the prisoners can take many steps to delay execution.

2. THE PROBLEM

The question here is whether a competent person convicted of a capital crime should have the right to forego any mandatory appeal and elect execution?[11] The argument weighing against the convict's autonomy interest arises from society's interest in assuring itself that the punishment it authorizes is just and right. This is important to preserve the moral authority of the

---

Sentenced" 24 *New Eng. J. on Crim & Civ. Confinement.* 279, 284-85 (1998). Seven of the states allowing capital punishment either do not require an automatic appeal of the conviction or allow the defendant to waive that appeal. None of the states permit waiver of the sentencing hearing. Idaho, Montana, South Dakota, and Tennessee require only review of the sentence; Indiana and Kentucky permit defendants to waive review of their conviction. South Carolina is the only state that does not require review of the sentence. Thomas P. Bonczar & Tracy L. Snell, *Bureau of Justice Statistics, Capital Punishment,* 2004 3 (2005). In Florida, death row volunteers may not waive the automatic appeals. They can proceed without counsel if they do not want to put on a mitigation defense to execution. George Judson, "Uniting to Seek a Death Penalty; Killer Works With Prosecutor on a New Sentence", *N.Y. Times,* 12 Dec 1995, at B1.

[8] Interview with John Clark, Attorney, in Palo Alto, Cal. (8 June 2006).

[9] "The prisoner's right to forego discretionary appeal has been consistently upheld." Kathleen L. Johnson, "The Death Row Right to Die: Suicide or Intimate Decision?" 54 *S. Cal. L. Rev.* 575, 576 (1981). *See Hammett v. Texas,* 448 U.S. 725 (1980); *Gilmore v. Utah,* 429 U.S. 1012 (1976); *Whitmore v. Arkansas,* 495 U.S. 149 (1990).

[10] Death Penalty Information Center, "Time on Death Row," http://www.deathpenaltyinfo.org/article.php?&did=1397 (last visited 16 July 2006).

[11] I assume a competent, psychologically well inmate under no compulsion to choose execution. Even among those found legally competent, many prison inmates suffer in a way that could influence their ability to make sound decisions. Nonetheless there are capable death row inmates who appreciate their own autonomy. *See Whitmore,* 495 U.S. at 165-66. I apply my argument to them.

criminal justice system[12] and to enforce constitutional limits on punishment.[13] Society suffers a distinct harm when it executes those who are factually innocent, whose convictions lack sanction under the law, or whose punishment should not be death. These societal interests are the stated justifications for mandatory appeals of capital convictions in cases where a defendant seeks immediate execution. Even if this justification is sufficient, the effect of mandatory appeals is that a guilty criminal's life belongs to the state; he or she loses the right to personal autonomy at the most basic level.[14]

State involvement distinguishes the circumstances of death volunteers from those of free persons seeking death with dignity. However, both present an issue of individual autonomy and the decision to die, therefore the medical world may offer some insights into how to respond to those who refuse to contest their sentences of death.

3. THE MEDICAL APPROACH

Contrast the death volunteer with a free person who is gravely ill. In the United States and certain other nations, patients may refuse treatment knowing that the effect of doing so will be to hasten death.[15] Oregon, Holland, Belgium, and

---

[12] J. Caleb Rackley, Comment: "Legal Ethics in Capital Cases: Looking for Virtue in Roberts v. Dretke and Assessing the Ethical Implications of the Death Row Volunteer," 36 *St. Mary's L.J.* 1119, 1148 (2005), citing Johnson, note 9, at 576.

[13] G. Richard Strafer, "Volunteering for Execution: Competency, Voluntariness and the Propriety of Third Party Intervention," 74 *J. Crim. L. & Criminology* 860, 896 (1983). *See also* Rackley, note 12, at 1148.

[14] Additional justifications for mandatory appeals include the states' traditional limit on personal autonomy to preserve life, as with mandatory motorcycle helmet laws. It also seeks to protect the adversarial process and the integrity of the legal profession. Some claim the state has an interest in preventing suicide, and distinguishes the right of the ill to die by the fact it is not the state killing. The state denies a defendant the right to choose his own punishment because that defeats the purpose of punishment. Rackley, note 12, at 1150-55.

[15] *In re Quinlan*, 70 N.J. 10, 39, 355 A.2d 647, 663 (1976). In Poland there is no statute permitting do-not-resuscitate instructions, but a terminally ill patient's expressed objection to continued

Switzerland allow people to elect assisted suicide.[16] All these jurisdictions, except Switzerland, impose certain conditions on a doctor before he or she may assist a patient to die. In general the laws require a person to have a terminal illness or great suffering and to make a voluntary, informed, persistent choice of death, where there is no acceptable alternative.[17] Thus both counseling and prediction are conditions of legal assistance with death. The Netherlands requires a neutral doctor's participation.[18] How would these standards apply to death volunteers?

3.1 Medical Counselling

Patients choosing to die should make a well-considered decision. To do so, the decider must have information about his or her alternatives. In the medical situation, the doctor presents this information about medical status, prognosis, and reasonable available alternatives, such as palliative care, in counseling the patient.[19] Moreover, all the states require

---

treatment is binding on his or her physician. Eleonora Zielinska, Patient's Autonomy Versus Physician's Autonomy in Polish Medical Law 13 (26 May 2006) (unpublished manuscript, on file with author).

[16] The laws vary in whether they permit only "voluntary euthanasia," that is the termination of life by a doctor at the patient's request, as in Belgium, or permit only "assisted suicide," meaning the patient takes the last step, as in Oregon and Switzerland. The Netherlands permits both. Switzerland and Holland do not limit the choice of death to the terminally ill as do Oregon and Belgium. By removing the decision to die from the question of illness, the Swiss make autonomy, rather than medical prognosis, the core value. In Switzerland anyone other than a doctor, can assist or incite suicide if acting with honorable motives and no self-serving interests. The title of the Oregon law, the "Death with Dignity Law," emphasizes the autonomy value at stake. *See Select Committee on the Assisted Dying for the Terminally Ill Bill, Report*, 2004-5, H.L. 86-1, at 54-73.

[17] The specific variations in the conditions are not significant in an examination of patient autonomy.

[18] The unique character of the Swiss law that gives a defense to a charge of assisting suicide for those who have no self-serving motives makes some of these conditions inapplicable. H.L. 86-1, note 16, at 69.

[19] *Id.* at 62.

the voluntary and durable decision of the patient,[20] evidenced in part by repeated requests. For example, in Belgium there must be several conversations between patient and doctor[21] and in Oregon, there must be two requests written 15 days apart followed by oral confirmation.[22] Thus the quality of a patient's well-considered decision depends on a doctor's careful, informative counseling.[23]

3.2 Medical Judgment

Implicit in most death-with-dignity laws is an expert prediction about the patient's future. In Belgium and Oregon, when a patient's medical condition is futile because of a terminal disease,[24] he or she may elect to end life.[25] Moreover, a patient may elect death in Belgium and The Netherlands when he or she is suffering unbearably.[26] "Unbearably" is an undefined phrase, which seems to imply biologically or psychologically persistent misery. This would make suffering

---

[20] *Id.* at 54-55, 61-62, 70-71, 73. Switzerland's non-governmental organizations that assist suicide set their own conditions but the ethical principles of the medical academy are consistent with the laws of other states. *Id.* at 70-71. Durability is important in the prison context where the majority of volunteers change their minds.

[21] *Id.* at 73.

[22] Or. Rev. Stat. §127.840 (2006). Upon conclusion of the 15 day waiting period Oregon law requires the physician "offer the patient the opportunity to rescind" the request and "verify, immediately prior to writing the prescription... that the patient is making an informed decision." Or. Rev. Stat. §127.815 (2006).

[23] Switzerland is an exception to this generalization. H.L. 86-I, note 16, at 69.

[24] *See, e.g.,* Or. Rev. Stat. 127.805 (2006). In Oregon the patient must expect to die within 6 months. Or. Rev. Stat. 127.800(12) (2006).

[25] H.L. 86-I, note 16, at 54, 73. In The Netherlands a doctor may assist with the death of a patient suffering biologically or psychologically. *Id.* at 61-62. This means a person could be terminally ill and not suffering, therefore ineligible for assistance. A focus on this biological approach to the right to life choice and to the American prohibition of voluntary euthanasia has driven academics to distinguish right to die issues from death volunteering. *See* John H. Blume, "Killing the Willing: "Volunteers," Suicide and Competency," 103 *Mich. L. Rev.* 939, 947 (2005)

[26] H.L. 86-I, note 16, at 61, 73.

more a function of the spirit than of the body. Switzerland goes further: no medical condition is necessary to justify assisted suicide[27] so some death assistance organizations will help healthy elderly persons who no longer see meaning in their life.[28] This approach privileges autonomy over prediction of death. It could apply to the death row volunteers who are suffering and see no meaning in their lives.

3.3 Neutral Professional

In Holland a doctor proposing to assist a patient's death must consult with another, independent doctor. After that doctor has visited the patient, he or she gives a written opinion on whether the treating physician has met the "due care" requirements, i.e. satisfied the legal conditions.[29] Certain doctors consult on death cases regularly[30] and thereby develop expertise in assisting the treating doctors and protecting patients.

4. THE LEGAL APPROACH

The three conditions characterizing death-with-dignity laws: counseling, judgment, and neutral professionals should apply to the lawyer-client relationship in death volunteers' cases.

4.1 Legal Counseling – The Obligation

A decision about something as profound as death depends on both the client and lawyer. Courts have found inmates to

---

[27] *Id.* at 70.

[28] *Id.* at 71.

[29] *Id.* at 62-63.

[30] The consulting doctor need not be from this specialized cadre. *Id.*

be competent to make binding, voluntary choices despite the stress of their situation.[31] The trickier issue is the quality of the convict's decision, which depends on the counseling he or she receives from his or her attorney.

The Model Rules of Professional Responsibility[32] impose on lawyers a duty to represent a client's interests within the law. To do this, an attorney must give every client all the information needed to make an informed decision. That requires a careful investigation of facts and law, and a clear presentation of alternatives from which the client may choose.[33] The client must understand this information and the important choice to be made. The parallel to a doctor-patient conversation is clear. After careful counseling, the American lawyer should vigorously advance the client's wishes or withdraw from representation. This duty places an attorney who opposes the death penalty and also believes in the client's right to decide in an uncomfortable position.[34]

The Model Rules do not address the subject of client autonomy in the context of death row volunteers. However, they do require a lawyer to respect the wishes of a client so long as those wishes are legal.[35] Rule 1.2(a) states that "a lawyer shall abide by a client's decisions concerning the objectives of representation."[36]

The United States Supreme Court has held that a defendant in a criminal case "has the ultimate authority to make certain

---

[31] *See Gilmore*, 429 U.S. at 1012 (1976); *Evans v. Bennett*, 440 U.S. 1301 (1979); *Hammett*, 448 U.S. at 725; *Lenhard v. Wolff*, 43 U.S. 1306 (1979).

[32] "[A]ll but eight of the jurisdictions [have] adopted new professional standards based on [the] Model Rules." Center for Prof. Responsibility, *A.B.A, Model Rules of Prof. Conduct* viii (2003).

[33] *See* Binder et al, *Lawyers as Counselors: A Client-Centered Approach* (2d ed. 2004).

[34] Thomas Ginsberg, "The Lesser Evil:Criminal Defense Lawyer Alan Zegas Opposes the Death Penalty. But His Client Wants to be Executed", *Philadelphia Inquirer*, 18 Aug. 1997, at D5.

[35] *Model Rules of Prof'l Responsibility* R.1.2(a) (2003).

[36] *Id.*

fundamental decisions regarding the case."[37] These decisions include "whether to plead guilty, waive a jury, testify in his or her own behalf, or take an appeal."[38] The inclusion of whether or not to appeal supports a death row volunteer's right to waive appeals. However, in cases involving waiver of appeals by those sentenced to death the Court has never specifically referenced the principle of individual autonomy. It has supported its decisions with arguments based on an inmate's ability to make competent decisions, which implies deference to personal autonomy.[39] In fact, the only conditions limiting a defendant's right to make substantive decisions are competency and that "the waiver of his constitutional rights is knowing and voluntary."[40] The trial court determines whether a defendant is acting in a "knowing and voluntary" manner.[41]

State courts have addressed the rights of death volunteers. In *People v. Lavalle*[42] a capital defendant refused to offer mitigating evidence during the sentencing phase of his trial. His lawyer tried to force the defendant to present mitigating evidence, claiming "to forego any mitigation would, in effect, result in a court-assisted suicide."[43] This argument was unsuccessful. The court determined that "[t]he decision whether to offer mitigation is one of those 'fundamental decisions' a defendant himself retains during the pendency

---

[37] *Jones v. Barnes*, 463 U.S. 745, 751 (1983).

[38] *Id.* at 751.

[39] The decision to allow the defendant to waive his appeals was based on his competence to make "a knowing and intelligent waiver of any and all federal rights." *Gilmore*, 429 U. S. at 1013.

[40] *Godinez v. Moran*, 509 U.S. 389, 400 (1993).

[41] *Id.* at 392-93.

[42] *N. Y. v. Lavalle*, 697 N.Y.S.2d 241 (1999).

[43] *Id.* at 242.

of his case," so long as he is competent.[44]

Such rulings indicate that the better interpretation of Rule 1.2(a) binds lawyers for death-sentenced criminal defendants to respect a client's wishes, even when they do not agree with a client's decision. As the court stated in *Lavalle*, "[w]hile some might question why a person would do what defendant wants to do, no one should question his right to do it."[45]

4.2 *Legal Counseling – The Practice*

It is difficult for a lawyer to follow ethical precepts when he or she can not accept the defendant's reason for choosing execution[46] and believes the client is doing him or herself harm. When the client is imprisoned on death row and the choice is to accept death, cool words, such as "difficult," do not adequately describe the drama of the lawyer's role.[47]

Under this pressure, the lawyers who represent death row inmates often do not present clients with their alternatives neutrally. In any criminal context, good counseling implies explaining to a client the legal avenues available, the probabilities of success, and the consequences of following each path. For example, choosing to exhaust all appellate opportunities *seriatim* may permit (or compel) the client to live a certain number of years. This is comparable to counseling by Dutch and Belgian doctors, during which the professionals present patients' "reasonable" alternatives,

---

[44] *Id.* at 242.

[45] *Id.* at 244.

[46] Death volunteers' explanations include committing the crime in order to get the death penalty, wanting to prevent killing again, wishing to preserve personal dignity, and sparing their family further agony. Richard C. Dieter, "Ethical Choices for Attorneys Whose Clients Elect Execution," 3 *Geo. J. Legal Ethics* 799, 803 (1990).

[47] *See generally* C. Lee Harrington, "A Community Divided: Defense Attorneys and the Ethics of Death Row Volunteering," 25 *Law & Soc. Inquiry* 849 (2000) (Interviews with 20 defense attorneys handling capital appeals).

including palliative care.[48] It is unlikely defense attorneys actually present their clients with the option of dropping all appeals in order to hasten their execution, even though that is permissible once the mandatory appeal is complete.

Some attorneys even misrepresent facts in vigorously opposing the client's wishes.[49] As one defense lawyer admitted:

> The truth remains that I lied to and manipulated a man who had entrusted me with his life.... [Imminent death] makes that man highly susceptible to coercion by his attorney.... By what right did I override my client's instructions? Once I had laid out... the risks and potential benefits, should I not have respected my client's wishes? It was, after all, his life.[50]

"Abolitionists," lawyers who adamantly oppose capital punishment on principle,[51] accept with dedication the too-often fruitless years of litigation to stave off executions. These lawyers work intensely to persuade their clients to challenge

---

[48] To show the autonomy interests underlying its legislation Belgium provides a patient cannot be compelled to accept palliative care and may choose death despite that option. H.L. 86-I, note 16, at 74.

[49] Welsh S. White, "Defendants Who Elect Execution," 48 *U. Pitt. L. Rev.* 853, 855-56, 860 (1987). *See* Harrington, note 47, at 869; *Brewer v. Lewis*, 989 F.2d 1021, 1023 (9th Cir. 1993) (Lawyer filed petition for *certiorari* to challenge Brewer's competency without his client's knowledge or consent.) In *Red Dog v. Delaware*, the defendant desired to waive further appeals in a capital case." 625 A.2d 245, 245-7 (1993). Nevertheless his lawyers requested a stay of execution to challenge their client's competency. *Id.* The court held this did not violate the rules of professional responsibility because the lawyers had "an objective and reasonable basis for believing that the client [could not] act in his own interest" and acted with in the best interests of the client. *Id.* However, the court criticized the lawyers for exercising "poor judgment" in refusing to accept their client's decision and cautioned them that lawyers are "not free to fashion [their] own code of ethics. *Id. See also Rees v. Peyton*, 384 U.S. 312 (1966) (*per curiam*). Not all dedicated capital defense lawyers are so adamant and most struggle with the conflict between saving an inmate's life and respecting his decision.

[50] Mello, Michael, "In the Years When Murder Wore the Mask of Law: Diary of a Capital Appeals Lawyer (1983 – 1986)," 24 *Vt. L. Rev.* 583, 709 (2000).

[51] *See* Johnson, note 9, at 589.

their convictions and sentences by all legal means.[52] "A defense lawyer's credo in a capital case generally is to exhaust every avenue to save an inmate's life."[53]

Criminal defense attorneys justify a paternal or maternal role that supersedes a death-sentenced client's autonomy in several ways. They are sometimes successful in saving a convict's life or even freeing a discouraged client.[54] They believe many murderers were "shortchanged by the justice system or they cannot be trusted to make their own decisions."[55] The difficulty of life on death row may destroy a client's capacity to make good decisions.[56] Many clients change their decision favoring death.[57] Finally, capital defense lawyers criticize colleagues who do represent a death volunteer's wishes, which may make client-centered lawyers leery about losing their professional support base.[58] Paradoxically the effect of

---

[52] Harrington, note 47, at 863-64.

[53] Howard Mintz, "Inviting Their Own Executions Faced With Long Appeals and Misery on Death Row Some Choose to Die Early. Experts are Divided on What Makes Death Row Inmates Abandon the Fight for Life as Robert Massie Becomes the Latest to End His Legal Fight," *San Jose Mercury News*, 4 Feb. 2001, at 1B. Prof. Robert Weisberg said some of these lawyers have the "simple goal to reduce executions, any way possible, and don't give a damn about the autonomy of the client, or not a big damn." Jane Gross, "Inmates Volunteering for Execution: California Killer's Case Fan Debate," *N.Y. Times*, 19 Aug. 1993, at A21.

[54] A comprehensive statistical investigation of capital case appeals and state and federal *habeas corpus* petitions in 26 states between 1973-1995 revealed 68% overturned the trial judgment. James S. Liebman, Jeffery Fagan & Valerie West, "A Broken System: Error Rates in Capital Cases, 1973-1995," 5 (12 June 2000), *at* http://www2.law.columbia.edu/instructionalserivices/liebman/liebman2.pdf, *reprinted in* James S. Liebman, Jeffery Fagan & Valerie West, "A Broken System: Error Rates in Capital Cases, 1973, 1995," 78 *Tex. L. Rev.* 1839 (2000) (abridged version of the original). After retrial, 7% of the defendants were acquitted and 82% were resentenced to less than death. *Id.* Another study of state reversals of capital cases in the same 26 states between 1990-1999 showed 39% of the reversals were of the conviction and 61% were reversals of sentences only. Barry Latzer & James N. G. Cauthen, "Capital Appeals Revisted," 84 *Judicature* 64, 67 (2000).

[55] Gross, note 53.

[56] Blume, note 25, at 950.

[57] The majority of volunteers do change their minds. O'Neill, note 3, at A1.

[58] Phillips, note 4; Harrington, note 47, at 878.

abolitionists' practices is to give us greater confidence that those clients who reject their lawyer's pressure and insist on execution are certain in their resolve to die.

4.3 Lawyer Judgment

Like patients who must be informed of their medical condition and prognosis, convicts should be fully informed about their legal condition. This includes hearing their lawyer's professional judgment of the likelihood that legal challenges or appeals will prevail.

A lawyer may conclude that legal challenges are futile.[59] Legal futility is not a biological state; it depends on a decision by court or governor. This invites an interesting question. Does a doctor have more certainty making a prognosis than a lawyer has predicting the results of judicial action? The doctor's decisions seem comparatively easy, despite the frequently-imagined possibility of discovering a "miracle cure." But imprecision in predicting judicial decisions should not deny every death volunteer the information needed to make a choice. One is very close to certainty in the case of a murderer who pleaded guilty and refused to participate in the sentencing hearing. That defendant has made his or her condition legally futile. Furthermore, the defendant may know much about his or her guilt—not about the legal errors but about moral guilt. The inmate surely knows more than the lawyers about his or her suffering and value system.

A client may reject his or her lawyer's judgment regarding procedural irregularities or constitutional errors and reasonably choose not to assert his or her rights. The decision to forego one's rights is implicit in personal autonomy. It denies convicts their humanity to insist that they cannot wish to atone or appreciate the wrongness of their acts,

---

[59] Even if an appeal is successful "the overwhelming majority... are eventually reconvicted and sentenced to imprisonment or death." *See* Latzer & Cauthen, note 54, at 65.

cannot desire to make a political statement, and cannot choose to live only meaningful lives in their own control.[60] On the other hand, an inmate may choose to endure terrible imprisonment for even a small chance to continue living or to be free. In any event, the defendant's decision will benefit from the attorney's professional judgment.

Inmates on death row suffer. They are locked in their cells for as much as 23 hours a day. They have little access to prison programs or other stimulation. They are isolated without human relationships.[61] One prisoner described death row as "a dehumanized hellhole of steel and concrete where the law of the jungle and degeneracy reign supreme."[62] Exhausting all appeals prolongs life in this environment.

Time is an important element in the consideration of the death volunteer's choice. The appellate process is extraordinarily slow, during which time the inmate must remain on death row.[63] This delay is justified to protect society's interest in fairness. Unfortunately, it is the inmate, imprisoned for an average of over 10 years[64] awaiting an execution, who bears the entire cost of protecting society's interest. Admittedly the citizenry pays to house and feed the inmate, but the amount of physical, psychological, and spiritual suffering endured on death row trivializes those expenditures. If we analogize to the situation of a terminally ill person, this process amounts to insisting he or she continue to suffer while medical science finishes all the tests of some potentially helpful

---

[60] Mintz, note 53.

[61] Blume, note 25, at 966.

[62] Johnson, note 9, at 601-02, (citing Robert Massie, "Death by Degrees," *Esquire*, April 1971, at 179-180).

[63] Extensive delay benefits those inmates who choose to challenge their convictions or sentences and wish to prolong their lives.

[64] Between 1977-1995 the average time between sentence and execution was 9 years, but rose to 10.6 years in 1989-1995. Liebman et al., note 54, at 10. According to the U.S. Dept of Justice, that time was 11 years in 2004. Bonczar & Snell, note 7, at 1.

novel treatment, despite the patient's desire for an end. That situation inspired the death-with-dignity movement.

Paradoxically, their suffering is given as a reason inmates are incapable of making well-considered decisions about execution;[65] but free patients' unbearable suffering is a justification for allowing them to choose death.

4.4 Neutral Legal Professional—A Proposal

A procedure comparable to the Dutch insistence that an independent doctor scrutinize each potential case of assisted suicide would improve the representation of death volunteers. An independent lawyer can evaluate the client's competence and the neutrality or fairness of the criminal defense lawyer's counseling to determine whether the client is making a voluntary, well-considered decision.[66] This should promote fair counseling and deter manipulation of the client. Even with this extra care, a death volunteer should be able to change his or her decision. The seriousness and irrevocability of execution justifies a special rule, even one inmates could exploit unfairly.[67]

The consultant could also evaluate the possibility of a successful legal challenge being filed on behalf of the inmate. These consulting lawyers must be experts in criminal law, especially death penalty issues, but would represent neither side in the litigation. The consultant would not do all the research and writing needed for an appeal to the Supreme Court, but should do good law work with the intellectual balance of academic writing. The consultant would not be ruling on the inmate's case. He or she would serve as a "reality

---

[65] Blume, note 25, at 950.

[66] The conversations between the consultant and the inmate and defense lawyer must be privileged. Similarly the consultant's opinion about the defendant's legal position must be protected from discovery by the prosecution or court.

[67] *See* Johnson, note 9, at 625.

check" on the defense counsel's prediction of success or failure. This proposal does not fit the adversarial system of American criminal justice, but is not unimaginable. A Washington state court judge, presented with the question of whether a death row inmate was making a "knowing, intelligent and voluntary" waiver of his appellate rights, appointed the defense counsel who the inmate had discharged to brief the potential appeals issues for the court.[68]

The death volunteer can combine the neutral evaluator's opinion and defense counsel's understanding of the law with his or her own knowledge of the facts of the case, measure of suffering, and personal values, when making a considered choice of execution or not. Given this level of certainty, society's demand for a thorough appeal can give way to the inmate's wish for dignity.[69] If we do not respect autonomy, we may "incarcerate the [defendant's] spirit—the one thing that remains free and which the state need not and should not imprison."[70]

5. CONCLUSION

The question whether United States jurisdictions should permit death volunteers to choose execution is inextricably intertwined with the purposes of capital punishment. If the purpose is to rid society of a criminal, there would be no objection to the death volunteers' request. If the purpose is to assure society that no innocent person is convicted, the present elaborate system of appeals and other challenges satisfies. If the purpose is retribution, denying prompt

---

[68] Jack Broom, "A Lawyer to Help Him Die: Attorney to Use Hearing in Try to Fulfill Dodd's Wish to be Executed," *Seattle Times*, 15 May 1991, at A1.

[69] Where the convicted person is challenging the propriety of the conviction and sentence there can be no such abbreviated review of the justness of capital punishment.

[70] *Lenhard ex rel. Bishop v. Wolff*, 603 F.2d 91, 94 (9th Cir.) (Sneed, J., concurring), stay of execution denied, *Lenhard* 444 U.S. at 807 (1979)(mem.).

execution to a death volunteer serves because it increases the convict's suffering by depriving the individual of autonomy.[71] It diminishes the quantity of societal vengeance to grant the request of a person convicted of a capital crime to be relieved from suffering by execution. This may explain why even a competent inmate, suffering on death row, who admits the correctness of his or her conviction and sentence, cannot exercise personal autonomy to choose death before mandatory appeal. To allow death row inmates a death with dignity does deny society some revenge, but reasserts the extremely important values of human dignity and autonomy.

---

[71] H.L. 86-I, note 16, at 28-29. (Prof. Glover recognized incarceration denies a person the right to die in Oregon).

Courts in Search of Legitimacy: the Case of Wrongful Life

Marc A. Loth

This discussion will consider how different courts deal with difficult cases, and how courts seek to maintain the legitimacy of their judicial authority. How do courts search for legitimacy? From what sources do they draw their legitimacy? As a central example, I will use what are often referred to as the "wrongful life" cases. These raise the question whether a medical care provider can be held liable for negligent malpractice that results in the creation or preservation of a life that is not considered worth living. This question touches upon the autonomy of the plaintiff. By comparing three judicial decisions in "wrongful life" cases from courts from the United States, France and the Netherlands I hope to illustrate different possible sources of judicial legitimacy.

As early as 1982 the Supreme Court of California had to decide a wrongful life case (*Turpin v. Sortini*).[1] The case was about two sisters – ironically named Hope and Joy Turpin – who both suffered from a hereditary hearing defect that robbed them of their hearing. Due to an incorrect diagnosis of Hope's hearing problems, her parents had already conceived Joy before they found out about Hope's true condition. They would not have wanted a second child had they known in advance that she too would suffer from this hereditary hearing defect. Mr. and Mrs. Turpin asked that the doctor, Sortini, be held liable for the wrongful life of Joy. The court declined

---

[1] *Turpin v. Sortini*, 31 Cal. 3d 220; 643 P.2d 954.

to do so on the ground that the damages could not be determined in any rational or reasoned fashion. That would involve comparison of the Joy's present condition with the
situation as it would be if she did not exist at all, which is – as
the court explained – "outside the realm of human competence." On the same ground, the court did sustain the claim
for extraordinary expenses for specialised teaching, training
and hearing equipment during her lifetime.

The French *Cour de cassation* twice addressed the wrongful
life issue, both in the same case of Nicolas Perruche.[2] This case
concerns a boy whose mother was infected with Rubella during her pregnancy, leading to serious neurological problems
for her son (deafness, partial blindness, and a heart condition;
symptoms of the so-called Gregg syndrome). The mother
was wrongly diagnosed, which deprived her of the option of
aborting her child (as she claims she would have chosen to
do). Though the appeals court had decided that the doctor and
the laboratory could not be held liable because there was no
causal connection between their wrongdoing and the claimed
damage (since that was the result of the Rubella infection),
the *Cour de cassation* overturned that decision and sent the
case to another appeals court. This court also decided that the
required causal link was missing and the case was again put
before the *Cour de cassation*. In the second Nicolas Perruche
decision, the *Cour* ruled that due to the negligence of the
doctor and the laboratory the mother was deprived of the
option of having her child aborted, and that the defendants
could be held liable for that wrongdoing. After a fierce public
debate, the legislator prohibited wrongful life claims across
the board. Damage can only be compensated when this
damage is a direct consequence of medical malpractice.

Only last year the Dutch *Hoge Raad* was confronted with

---

[2] *Cour de cassation*, Nicolas Perruche 1 and 2 (26 March 1996, D. 1997, Jur. P. 35, 17 November 2000, D. 2001, Jur. P. 332).

a wrongful life case.[3] During her pregnancy, the mother consulted her midwife because there had already been two cases of handicaps due to a chromosome disorder in her husband's family. The midwife did not think it necessary to investigate the matter any further. This was later regarded as having been a professional failure with dramatic effects. Once born, baby Kelly turned out to have both mental and physical handicaps from which she suffered severely. The parents claimed damage – both on their own accord and in the name of Kelly – and their claims were sustained by both the appeals court and the *Hoge Raad*. The *Hoge Raad* not only addressed the legal issues but also considered moral and pragmatic arguments that had been put forward against wrongful life claims. First, there is the moral worry that sustaining such claims would violate the principle of the dignity of human life, by implying that having not been born would be preferable to living in a condition like this. Second, there is the pragmatic argument that sustaining claims such as this will tempt doctors to practice "defensive medicine" to avoid serious risk. Both arguments were carefully examined and rejected. The decision has been well accepted by the general public.

Here we have three cases of "wrongful life," decided by three different courts, in different ways on different grounds. The purpose of giving these examples is not to examine the fine details of arguments for and against wrongful life claims, but rather to address the question of how courts search for legitimacy in answering difficult questions. Mitchell Lasser recently published an interesting book in which he compared the *Cour de cassation*, the United States Supreme Court and the European Court of Justice (ECJ), thus drawing experience from different legal systems.[4] Lasser's approach combines

---

[3] *Hoge Raad* 18 March 2005, LJN:AR5213

[4] Lasser, Mitchel, *Judicial Deliberations: A Comparative Analysis of Judicial Transparency and Legitimacy*. Oxford: Oxford University Press, 2004.

the discursive and the institutional dimensions of the courts under investigation, showing us connections which were heretofore unnoticed. His analysis does not, however, recognize the functional dimension of the courts, which is an important third element in their relation to legitimacy. This concerns the actual role that courts play in the legal order and in society at large. The most effective frame of analysis will give due attention to three different dimensions of legitimacy: the discursive, the institutional, and the functional dimensions of legitimacy (or, stated alternatively, the argumentative, organizational, and social aspects of legitimacy). The specific arrangements that are responsible for the legitimacy of a specific court can be analyzed as specific combinations of discursive, institutional and functional variables. To illustrate this hypothesis I will elaborate on the examples introduced, replacing for general purposes the Supreme Court of California with the United States Supreme Court (since the differences are not relevant in this context).

TWO OPPOSITES: *COUR DE CASSATION* AND THE UNITED STATES SUPREME COURT

1. *COUR DE CASSATION*

It is not unusual among comparatists to present the French *Cour de cassation* and the US Supreme Court as opposites.[5] The *Cour de cassation* is held to be rather formalistic, because of its short decisions, which are syllogistic in structure and magisterial in tone. The US Supreme Court, on the other hand, is considered to be pragmatic, because of its extensively personally and politically motivated decisions. These differences are there, not to be ignored, but the picture is more complex than this simple opposition suggests.

---

[5] For the background of the respective different legal systems I recommend Glenn, H. Patrick. *Legal Traditions of the World.* Oxford: Oxford University Press, 2000.

Lasser relativizes this opposition from both sides. On closer inspection it seems rather unfair to depict the French judiciary as formalistic. In addition to the formal-seeming structured judicial decisions, there is also an unofficial discourse which is constituted by the opinions of the Advocates General, the annotations of legal scholars, and the reports of the reporting magistrates.[6] Though the results of this discourse are discussed in a public hearing and not always published, it is here that the real debate takes place. In this (partly) hidden discourse, an intense debate can be pursued concerning equity, substantive justice, and the contemporary needs of society.

This debate is channelled through recognized legal forms, such as precedents, interpretations, and the opinions of scholars, but is in reality an open-ended, equity-oriented and personal debate, in which all the arguments that are lacking in the official discourse are exchanged. As such, it provides a necessary complement to the official discourse, which could not exist in the form that it does without the sheltered parallel debate pursued in the unofficial discourse. The unofficial discourse provides the insights, arguments and points of view, on the basis of which the *Cour de cassation* makes its laconic decisions. These authorized interpretations of law reappear in the decisions in their typical formalized, syllogistic, and ritualized forms. Actually, it is the established division of labour between the two spheres of discourse that makes the system work, attributing the real debate to the unofficial discourse, and reserving the authorized decision-making to the *Cour* itself. This advances the efficiency of the system by making it possible for the *Cour de cassation* (162 judges and 27 Advocates-General) to deal with a caseload of 30,000 to 35,000 cases a year.[7]

---

[6] *Supra* note 4.

[7] www.courdecassation.fr (L'activité de la Cour, statistique année 2004). The 162 judges, 27 advocates general, and 18 legal writers, are divided over 6 chambers: 3 civil chambers, 1

But does the *Cour de cassation* also serve the legitimacy of the system? From what sources does the court draw its legitimacy? The French system relies mainly on institutional sources to generate judicial legitimacy.[8] Lasser explains that the judicial system is firmly anchored in the political system by which French society shapes itself. Several of these anchors can be mentioned. First, there is the strict separation of the judicial system from the political system, secured by the separation of powers, the theory of sources of law which secures the supremacy of legislation, and a methodology of strict law application. Of course this separation is backed by a rather positivistic legal theory, in which a strict division is maintained between the domain of facts and that of the values.[9] Second, there is a state-formed elite of magistrates (and law professors, for that matter), selected and educated on a meritocratic basis. They form, so to speak, the human flesh on the skeleton of the judicial system. Thirdly, this elite has a republican ethos of service to the state, in the name of the general public interest. This ethos presupposes a right answer to difficult legal questions which can be discussed, discovered and authoritatively given by the state-formed elite of judges and magistrates (reminiscent of Plato's "philosopher-kings").[10]

This socio-institutional arrangement has provided judicial legitimacy thus far, as Lasser shows, but it can be questioned whether it will continue to do so in the foreseeable future. To explain this we have to take his analysis beyond the discursive and institutional level to consider the functional aspects of legitimacy. This perspective reveals three possible risks for

---

commercial, 1 social, and 1 criminal chamber.

[8] *Supra* note 4.

[9] This was the prevailing legal theory in the days of the formation of the *Code Civil* (1804), which is up until this day the most important legal source for the *Cour de cassation* and the French judiciary in general.

[10] *Supra* note 4.

the French answer to the question of judicial legitimacy. The first is that the separation of the judicial and the political system is increasingly difficult to uphold in modern West-European legal systems.[11] As Guarnieri and Pederzoli have shown in an extensive comparative study, the judiciary plays an increasingly important political role, which raises new issues of legitimacy (such as "who guards the guardians?").[12] This places the judges in West-European legal systems, including France, more in the forefront of controversial political issues.

The second risk is that in a pluralistic society it is increasingly difficult to build legitimacy on a shared conception of substantive justice, to be discovered by a legal elite. This is true not only because people are becoming less inclined to put trust in legal elites, but also because substantive justice gives way to procedural justice. What is considered to be the right outcome of legal proceedings is not so much the right answer, in any objective sense, but rather the result of a fair trial in which all parties have had their due. Finally, it has been noticed that citizens in modern society put their trust less in input-legitimacy, and turn increasingly to output-legitimacy.[13] If this is true, it means that judicial legitimacy depends less on factors such as institutional independence or the selection, recruitment and training of judges, than it does on factors such as the quality of the proceedings, decisions, motivations, communication, and the like. It is the performance of the judiciary that counts, rather than its position in society. Of course, this relativizes the French institutional answer to the question of legitimacy.

---

[11] The same applies to its different parts, such as the separation of powers, the methodology of law application and the positivistic separation of facts and law.

[12] Carlo Guarnieri and Patrizia Pederzoli. *The Power of Judges: A Comparative Study of Courts and Democracy*. Oxford: Oxford University Press, 2002.

[13] Wetenschappelijke Raad voor het Regeringsbeleid (WRR), *De toekomst van onze nationale rechtsstaat*, The Hague 2002, p. 110.

2. UNITED STATES SUPREME COURT

Let us turn now to the other extreme and the United States
Supreme Court. The U.S. system is characterized by a unified,
integrated discourse in the form of the judicial opinion.
These opinions are well known for their anti-formalism. This
is illustrated by the decisions of the United States Supreme
Court. The sheer length of the decisions – which can take
some 20 or more pages – suggests an extensive argumentat-
ion in a dialogical form. Characteristic of these decisions is
a heavily fact-oriented analysis, in which the judges devote
considerable effort to describing the factual circumstances of
the case. This is not just a starting point for the application
of the law, but also as an exemplification of a realistic
orientation in the law, in which legal consequences depend
largely on their purposes and effects. The consequences of
the decisions, more than the court's rationale, seem to be the
determining factor in the decision-making process. This is
all written down in a very personal style, in which the legal
ethos of the judge can easily be recognized. The individual
judicial responsibility is strengthened, of course, by the
personal signature of the judge under the majority decision,
as well as by the possibility of concurring and dissenting
opinions. Each judge is accountable for both his or her
personal decisions as well as for his or her arguments in each
individual decision. Therefore it is in the first place the judge
speaking, not the court or the judiciary.[14] On the other hand,
the opinion transcends sheer pragmatism, because policy
arguments are channelled through formal means, such as
judicial tests, rules of thumb, legal principles, precedents,
and the like. To accuse an American judge of engaging in
politics is as serious a criticism as to blame him or her of
formalism.

---

[14] The high profile of the nine judges of the Supreme Court is illustrated by their curricula on the
Supreme Court's website. *See* www.supremecourtus.gov.

The Supreme Court is notorious for its ethos of independence. President Eisenhower famously stated: "During my presidency I have made two mistakes, and they are both sitting in the Supreme Court." This illustrates the extent to which the Supreme Court (unlike the *Cour de cassation*) plays an outspoken political role through its power of constitutional review.[15] The discourse in which the judiciary participates can be characterized as both anti-formalistic and anti-policy, or – to put it the other way around – it has both formal and pragmatic aspects. The judicial discourse is largely an autonomous one, which constitutes a separate interpretive, argumentative, hermeneutic discourse.[16]

From what sources does the Supreme Court draw its legitimacy? The Supreme Court draws mainly from discursive sources to generate judicial legitimacy.[17] Several anchors embed this practice firmly in the judicial system, as Lasser shows. First, there is the doctrine of case law, which supplies each judicial decision with a recognized legal purpose. In that sense, the legislator and the judiciary are "partners in the business of law." The emphasis is not so much on the doctrine of the separation of powers, as it is on the balance of powers ("checks and balances"). Second, there is the theory and practice of explaining and justifying case law by argumentative means, to an ever-increasing level of detail. This contributes not only to the understanding and acceptance of the decision by the parties, but also to a context of judicial accountability and transparency towards society at large. In broader terms, this "good reasons approach" serves both an informational and an educational purpose, and forms an exemplary illustration of what judicial decision-making and responsibility can and should be. The discourse of the

---

[15] Which in France is attributed to the *Conseil constitutionnel*.

[16] Which deals with an increasing caseload: 1460 cases on the docket in 1945, 2313 in 1960, and more than 7000 nowadays (*see* www.supremecourtus.gov).

[17] *Supra* note 4.

Supreme Court is an integrated discourse with a plurivocal cacophonic sound, since each judge has his or her own voice. This system exemplifies the ideas of practical rationality and procedural justice in a democratic system, showing that there is not one right answer (to be discovered and authorized by a judiciary elite), but that there are several options that can be defended on good grounds. In a democratic society this seems preferable, simply because more people recognize their views and convictions in the motivations of the courts.

Are there no drawbacks for the American system then? According to Lasser there are, because there is no alternative discourse as in France.[18] There are no Advocate Generals opinions and the academic commentary is banished to the law reviews. This may be a trivial difference because there is enough opportunity for difference of opinion within this integrated discourse itself (as through the possibility of concurring and dissenting opinions). The analysis must be taken a step further to understand the real problem, which arises from the vulnerability of judicial discourse in relation to political influence. The ongoing debate on judicial restraint or activism shows permanent awareness of the political role of the Supreme Court. This is reflected in the political character of the appointment of judges in the Supreme Court. Because of this, the independence of the judges is dependent on their ethos, which is not a very strong safeguard. The case of *Bush vs. Gore* illustrated this problem by dividing the Supreme Court along party lines. This reveals how important it is that judicial discourse remains firmly rooted in a strong institutional setting. While the Supreme Court is strong in discursive sources of legitimacy, it is weak in institutional sources. The *Cour de cassation* is just the opposite. From this perspective, they are mirror images of each other.

---

[18] *Supra* note 4.

3. THE EUROPEAN COURTS AS IN-BETWEENS

3.1 *European Court of Justice (ECJ)*

A similar analysis can be extended to the European courts. From this standpoint both the European Court of Justice and the European Court of Human Rights take an in-between position between the opposites already discussed, but each in a different way. The ECJ is characterized by Lasser as a hybrid which originated as an offspring of its model, the *Cour de cassation*, but with Anglo-American overtones.[19] As in the French example, the ECJ encompasses two discursive spheres: the official discourse of the decisions of the ECJ and the unofficial sphere of the opinions of the Advocate Generals and the annotations of legal commentators. As in the French case, the distinction is based on a division of labour between authoritative decision-making and substantive debate. The rulings of the ECJ are the result of collegial decision-making. They suggest logical compulsion and are written in an impersonal style. Lasser stresses that they differ from the decisions of the *Cour de cassation*, however, in that they use purposive arguments in considering the EU treaties as a whole, seeking to advance the effectiveness of community law, the requirements of legal certainty and uniformity, the legal protection of individual community rights, and finally: the system of the treaty. Thus, the ECJ tries to improve the French example on the discursive level, by allowing for more extensive motivations. In this respect, the ECJ resembles the United States Supreme Court, but there is a fundamental difference. Because of the dialogue with precedents and its factual character, the motivation behind the decisions of the Supreme Court reaches an ever-increasing level of detail, while the motivations of the ECJ remain at a rather abstract

---

[19] The ECJ consists of 25 judges (1 per member state of the EU) and 8 Advocate Generals, organized in chambers of 3 or 5 judges, or a grand chamber of 13 judges. In 2004, they dealt with 665 cases, 531 new ones, and 840 pending (in 2000: 526, 503, and 873 respectively). *See* www.curia.eu.int. The court of first instance is not taken into consideration.

level. This reflects the different responsibility of the ECJ, which is to build a legal system on the provisions of the Treaties. As Tim Koopmans writes: "The Court had to feel its way. It did so by deriving some basic rules from the multiplicity of technical provisions, by interpreting these rules in the light of the aims of the treaty, and by slowly developing a system of case law on that foundation."[20]

Bengoetxea has drawn a similar, but more precise picture than Lasser. The ECJ is in his words "very Dworkinian," "taking the European Community project seriously and making the best and most coherent story of European integration which is embodied in that project."[21] The ECJ makes use of different kinds of methods of interpretation and reasoning, mainly (i) semiotic or linguistic arguments (divergence between different language versions, ordinary language), (ii) systematic and contextual arguments (in situations of gap or antinomy: the *sedes materiae* argument and quasilogical arguments such as the argument *per analogiam, a fortiori, a pari, lex specialis, lex superior, a contrario,* conceptual arguments, and teleo-systematic arguments), and (iii) teleological, functional or consequentialist arguments (the apagogic argument, the weighing and balancing of principles, policy arguments).[22] In general, preference is given to systematic-functional criteria ("a systematic-cum-dynamic-interpretation"), as is shown for example in the ruling in the case of *Van Gend and Loos* (in which the object of the Treaty and Article 177 justify the conclusion that Community law has an authority which can be invoked by their nationals, from which it follows that if the Treaty imposes obligations on individuals and Member States, it must also confer rights on individuals). The frequent

---

[20] Koopmans, Tim. *Courts and Political Institutions*: A Comparative View. Cambridge: Cambridge University Press, 2003, p. 89.

[21] Bengoetxea, Joxerramon. *The Legal Reasoning of the European Court of Justice*: Towards a European Jurisprudence. Oxford: Oxford University Press, 1993. p. vi and 99.

[22] *See Id* at 233-270.

appeal to the system of the Treaties and the aims they pursue makes us aware that "in doing so the Court is engaging in a special form of social action, furthering the aims of the Treaties by recourse to dynamic criteria and reconstructing the EC law into a coherent and consistent whole by recourse to systematic criteria."[23] This is done in favour of the overall objective of obtaining legitimacy for the EC and its law: "Using contextual and systematic criteria of interpretation can thus be seen as a form of social action whereby the Court seeks to obtain legitimacy and adherence to a body of norms."[24]

The sought-after legitimacy extends not only to the law of the EC, but also to its institutions, including the Court itself: "The relevance of the Court's justification of its own decisions lies in the attempt to achieve legitimacy amongst the audiences to which such justifications are addressed. The making legitimate of the European Community idea of an ever closer union is thus an internal process assumed by the judges of the ECJ before their audiences."[25] From this we can conclude that the discursive legitimacy the ECJ seeks to establish in its rulings is closely connected to the formation of the European community as a whole and the process of European integration. Recent developments have shown that this makes the ECJ vulnerable when the project of European integration becomes unpopular or even suspect for the general public. At the end of the day, the legitimacy of the ECJ shares the fate of that of the other EU institutions and even of the political process of European integration, embedded as it is in the institutions and the formation of the European Community.

---

[23] *See id.* at 234.

[24] *See id.* at 98.

[25] *See id.* at 99.

3.2 *European Court of Human Rights (ECHR)*

Although the ECHR had to build a legal discourse from scratch, as did the ECJ, the starting-point was rather different. In the words of Tim Koopmans: "The provisions of the European Convention are not very technical, but rather general and vague. In order to make the provisions workable, the European Court had to break them up into three or four 'sub-standards' which were practicable and which could, in their turn, lead to further ramifications."[26] The ECHR succeeded in creating a lively and effective discourse on human rights, and the question arises how this can be explained. One of the explanations is perhaps that the human rights discourse of the ECHR is, in terms of Lasser, a unified discursive context. The majority decisions of the Court, dealing with the alleged violation of one of the provisions of the European treaty on human rights, speak with one voice. They are the result of collegial decision-making and are formulated in an impersonal tone ("the Court"). The rulings of the court are rather long, containing extensive descriptions of the procedure, the facts (the circumstances of the case and the relevant domestic law), and the law (the applicants complaints, the alleged violations, and the court's assessment), resulting in the decision. Debate is stimulated by the possibility of concurring and (jointly or partly) dissenting opinions, which display a more personal tone (such as "I," "we" and "in my view") arguing why the majority decision is supposed to be wrong. There is no institute such as the Advocate Generals advising the court, but there is a lively tradition of legal scholars discussing the case law of the Court, both on a national and an international level. All in all, the discourse organizes a rather lively discussion on the meaning and extension of the human rights provisions of the treaty.

---

[26] *Supra* note 20.

The ECHR owes its legitimacy partly to the transparency and the accountability of its rulings. If the ECJ can be characterized as "a Dworkinian Court," then the ECHR surely can. In building a human rights discourse on the basis of a single treaty, Koopmans writes, "the European Court thereby explicitly accepted the idea of legal evolution in the area of human rights protection, and the role of the judiciary in drawing conclusions from it. That attitude may have contributed to the more or less activist character of much of the European Court's case law."[27] Only recently the ECHR confirmed its conviction that the Treaty is a living document, to be interpreted in the light of present-day opinions.[28] Although it has been said that the ECJ too plays an activist role, there is a notable difference. Starting in the economic area, the ECJ has built a new legal system of a somewhat technocratic nature, which has not attracted a lot of public attention.[29] The ECHR on the other hand, created a discourse on human rights with remarkable results, which did arouse a lot of public attention and support. Besides, the case law of the ECHR has proved to be a vehicle for social, legal and political change in most of the members of the Council of Europe. The case law of the ECHR has initiated major legal reforms in the Member States, in private law, criminal law, as well as in administrative law. The ECHR can be addressed by individual citizens when all national legal means are exhausted, which makes the court very accessible for individual citizens and activist lawyers. This, more than anything else, has contributed to the legitimacy of the ECHR. The success of the ECHR can be measured by the enormous growth in the caseload, which increased from some 5,979

---

[27] *Surpa* note 20.

[28] ECHR 13 July 2004, nr. 69498/01, NJ 2005, 508.

[29] *Supra* note 21.

cases in 1998 to 13,858 cases in 2001.[30] Proposals for judicial reform are in discussion now, intended to rescue the court from its own success. Another risk is that certain Member States of the Council of Europe have developed an attitude of non-compliance to the rulings of the court (most notably Russia). This could weakens the court's legitimacy. Lastly, it should be noticed that the input-legitimacy of the ECHR is rather weak. The judges are appointed from the 45 Member States by the Parliamentary Assembly, for a period of 6 years.[31] For both the ECJ and the ECHR the idea and practice of national representation makes the legitimacy of the courts vulnerable. In hard cases citizens could respond to the rulings of both European courts with the question: why should we accept a ruling that is given by politically appointed judges from until recently unknown countries? The future will teach us whether the European courts can afford to ignore this criticism or whether institutional reform will be necessary.

3.3 The Dutch Hoge Raad

Let us return to the national courts, in this case the Dutch *Hoge Raad*. As in the cases of the ECJ and the ECHR, the *Hoge Raad* can be characterized as falling between the two extremes, in the sense that it draws its legitimacy both from institutional and discursive factors. Let us examine them individually. On the institutional level, the *Hoge Raad* is comparable to the *Cour de cassation* and is in fact, historically, a copy of the French system. Both are courts of cassation in civil and criminal cases, dealing only with questions of law (not questions of fact). As such they are not to be understood as third instance courts (next to the courts of first instance and the appellate courts), but rather

---

[30] European Court of Human Rights, informatienoot van de griffier 2004, p.3. *See* www.echr. coe.int..

[31] There are 45 judges; one judge for each party to the treaty. They are organized in 4 sections formed for 3 years, each of which contains committees of 3 judges for 1 year. Additionally, there are chambers of 7 judges, and the grand chamber of 17 judges (www.echr.coe.int).

as offering a form of judicial review (checking whether the law is correctly applied). "The principal role of a Supreme Court is to give authoritative rulings on the law," John Bell writes, and as such they fulfil a national role (distinct from the regional role of appeal courts).[32]

In this line the primary responsibility of the *Hoge Raad* is to serve the uniformity of the legal system, for which task it is given a position at the top of the judicial hierarchy for civil and criminal adjudication (administrative adjudication is attributed to another hierarchy with the Council of State at the top). In playing this unifying role the *Hoge Raad* fulfils two other functions attributed by law, namely the legal protection of the parties involved, and the creation of law. This last function requires more explanation since according to the doctrine of the separation of powers (*Trias Politica*) it is supposed to be the legislature which makes the law, and the judiciary that applies the law. In the Netherlands this doctrine of the separation of powers is less strictly applied than in France, since it is an acknowledged fact that judicial lawmaking is both necessary (interpretation involves the creation of new law) and desirable (judicial lawmaking keeps the law up to date). This more flexible approach to the relation between the legislature and the judiciary – more as a balance of powers than as a separation of powers – is completed with a less positivistic, more hermeneutic approach by judges. The *Hoge Raad* and in fact the judiciary as a whole, is seen as being engaged in the interpretation of evolving law in individual cases, which involves the mutual adjustment of facts and norms. This picture was already sketched by an influential pre-war Dutch scholar (Paul Scholten), and it resembles the Dworkinian picture of judicial adjudication far better than the positivistic model.[33]

---

[32] Bell, John. *Reflections on Continental European Supreme Courts. Legal Studies* (2004) 160.

[33] Scholten, Paul. *Algemeen Deel.* Zwolle 1974(2).

As a result, the case law of the *Hoge Raad* is *de facto* a source of law, in the sense that is in fact authoritative for other courts (not *de iure* since it is not legally binding). Both the *Hoge Raad* itself and the lower courts tend to follow its case law, both on legal grounds (equality) and for pragmatic purposes (saving parties the trouble of cassation). Though the doctrine of *stare decisis* is not formally in place in the Netherlands, adjudication can be regarded as an ongoing dialogue with precedents. In this dialogue, not only the *Hoge Raad* and the lower courts play their part, but also the Advocates General with their conclusions in each case in cassation and the legal scholars with their annotations. The distinction Lasser makes between the official discourse of the rulings of the court and the unofficial discourse of the conclusions and annotations is to be made in the Dutch context as well, though less strictly. As we saw, in France the substantial debate takes place in unofficial discourse, while the *Cour de cassation* presents its authoritative choice from among the discussed alternatives in a syllogistic form and in a magisterial tone. In the Netherlands, the division of labor between the official and the unofficial discourse is somewhat more vague, because the *Hoge Raad* plays an active role in the discussion of matters of substantial justice, equity and social needs. Its reasoning contains interpretive arguments and deliberations made on moral grounds and with regard to the factual consequences.

The case of baby Kelly provides a useful illustration, since in its ruling the court addressed legal arguments, the principle of the dignity of human life, and the possible consequences of the decision itself (see paragraph 1). This took some 12 pages, next to the 28 pages of the conclusion of the Procurar General. One can say that the *Hoge Raad* – in comparison with the *Cour de cassation* – has improved both the quality and quantity of its reasoning. In this ambition to improve on its reasoning the *Hoge Raad* resembles more the United States Supreme Court than the *Cour de cassation*. In other words, in its output the *Hoge Raad* aspires to emulate the American example, while its input continues to reflect its French origin. This is the characteristic middle position of the *Hoge Raad*, between two opposites.

3.4 Comparing the Wrongful Life Cases

This comparison of French, American, European, and Dutch courts establishes a perspective from which to examine the "wrongful life" cases. Apart from its outcome, the Supreme Court of California ruling is the most convincing. It is a reasoned reflection on the precedents available, the legislation at hand and the principles involved, with a due regard for the choices left to be made. It is clear in the questions to be answered ("This case presents the question of whether a child born with an hereditary affliction may maintain a tort action against a medical care provider who – before the child's conception – negligently failed to advise the child's parents of the possibility of the hereditary condition, depriving them of the opportunity to choose not to conceive the child") and it is cautious in the policies accepted ("we cannot assert with confidence that in every situation there would be a societal consensus that life is preferable to never having been born at all"). It is directed to the parties involved and the public at large and it is written in comprehensible language (here and there even in a literary style). It reflects differences of opinion by the simultaneous publication of concurring and dissenting opinions, thus showing that the plurality of opinions in society on such a complicated moral issue is reflected within the court, though on higher legal ground. As mentioned before, this does more justice to the ideas of practical reason and procedural justice than the alternative: one authorized opinion, arrived at through voting in chambers.

The first approach is more convincing, as it signals that the ruling rests on solid grounds, and not only on the authority of a specific court. As such, the ruling is an example of horizontal authority, not of vertical authority. This is more effective in a society where the authority of institutions is no longer taken for granted, but has to be earned on each occasion of performance. Are there no drawbacks then for the methods of California Supreme Court? I think there are, but they cannot be read from the court's rulings. As we mentioned in the context of the US Supreme Court, they are of an institutional nature. Though there are different procedures for the appointment of judges in state courts and in federal courts, both are subject to political influence. This makes these courts vulnerable, perhaps not so much to direct political control (which is tempered by the judicial ethos of independence), as to the more indirect influence of political criticism (which is hard to redress).

Compare this picture with the French approach in the cases of Nicolas Perruche. In very short, syllogistically structured rulings the *Cour de cassation* "dictated" its decision. This decision was far less convincing. We can hardly find any reasons for the decision, nor is there substantial deliberation on precedents and principles. What we do find is an unclear structure in which deliberations are tied to means of cassation ("moyen des cassation"), deliberations are put in the indirect mode ("Que..."), and where the decision is delivered (not reasoned). It is not surprising in a controversial matter such as this that the ruling (after being committed) failed to convince even the appeals court (which made the exceptional step of following the first appellate court instead of the *Cour de cassation*).

Neither is it surprising that in France the question of the admissibility of wrongful life claims was eventually not decided by the judiciary, but by the legislature. Of course, one can say that this is very much the French way of doing things, since it fits the model of the *Trias Politica*. This is true, but one can hardly maintain that this contributes to the legitimacy of the *Cour de cassation*. As the case of the ECHR has shown, the social, moral and political role a court plays can be of crucial importance for its legitimacy. A lack of social relevance can be damaging for judicial legitimacy. When the *Cour de cassation* aspires to be a relevant institution in present day French society it has to reconsider its ways of dealing with important questions like this. Otherwise it runs the risk of being marginalized. On a more abstract level, the French case illustrates the extent to which legitimacy depends on functional variables. This vindicates the extension of Lasser's approach to embrace functionality.

What about the *Hoge Raad* ruling in the case of baby Kelly? The extensively reasoned judgement was far more convincing than those of the *Cour de cassation*, but in comparison with the ruling of the Californian court some weaknesses remained. First, though the decision was supported by reasoning, this was done in only one voice (because there were no concurring or dissenting opinions). Therefore the ruling does not reflect the diversity of opinions that exist in society when considering such a controversial matter like this, as does the Californian ruling did, because it allowed dissents. As has been explained this seems a serious drawback, both from the perspective of democracy and of transparency. The *Hoge Raad* succeeded in fulfilling its role as a moral/legal guide for public debate, but more in the manner of Plato's "philosopher king." In a modern society the moral role of a court such as the *Hoge Raad* will be more relevant if it reflects the diversity of opinions in society within the court itself. Second, though the ruling in the case of baby Kelly did refer to the moral principle of the dignity of human life, it did not really succeed in integrating this principle in the legal reasoning. What do I mean by this?

As has been mentioned, the *Hoge Raad* sustained the claim of the parents (both on their own accord and in the name of Kelly), and did not consider this a violation of the principle of the dignity of human life. On the contrary, the *Hoge Raad* concluded that sustaining the claim would better serve that purpose, but putting Kelly in a better position to lead a bearable life. This is a truism, of course, but it misses the point of the argument. In making this suggestion, the *Hoge Raad* transforms the argument from a general principle that justifies a legal decision into a specific goal that is realised by a legal decision. As such it justifies too much, implying that every claim must be sustained, because this will put the complainant in a better position to lead a fulfilling human life. The *Hoge Raad* made this mistake because it addressed this moral principle directly, without the mediation of legal sources. Where the *Cour de cassation* was too exclusive, refusing to consider the moral merits of the case, the *Hoge Raad* was too inclusive. The first approach is not convincing in a case with such important moral overtones as this one, the second case is not convincing in a society which is so morally divided as ours. Both considerations must be taken into account by courts if they hope to maintain their legitimacy.

4. CONCLUSIONS

Where does this leave us? After introducing the case of wrongful life we considered the sources from which different courts draw their legitimacy in dealing with hard cases such as this. This revealed, first, the contrast between the rather formalized, short, syllogistic, magisterial decisions of the French *Cour de cassation*, and the pragmatic, long, dialogical, personal decisions of the United States Supreme Court justices. The French system seems to rely on input-factors as dominant sources for judicial legitimacy (institutional legitimacy), while the Supreme Court draws its legitimacy from discursive means (discursive legitimacy). This situation is strengthened by a different organisation of the debate. The French system displays a bifurcation with an emphasis on the unofficial discourse as the context for the real debate, while in the American system the debate takes place within the court itself (as is shown by majority and minority opinions).

For Europeans the difference is relevant, because the French system is mimicked in the ECJ, while the American system is copied by the ECHR. As has been argued, the latter system seems preferable in a modern democracy, where substantive justice and social elitism have given way to procedural justice and meritocracy.

The European courts seem to take in-between positions, as they each display a unique mixture of output- and input-legitimacy. The ECJ has built up a legal system based on the EU Treaties, interpreting them and other EU provisions in a Dworkinian fashion in the best possible way to advance European integration. As Bengoetxea writes, "the ECJ has 'une certaine idée de l'Europe'." The consequence is that the legitimacy of the ECJ is connected with the European integration as a whole, which is not without risk, as recent developments show. The ECHR has developed a human rights discourse on the basis of the Treaty of Rome (1950), also interpreting it in a Dworkinian fashion. Its activism has been more successful than that of the ECJ, because the topics dealt with speak more to the mind (are less technocratic), have had a large positive impact on the legal systems of the Member States. The legitimacy of the ECHR is not to be taken for granted however, because the Court has serious problems both with caseload and compliance. Finally, there is the issue of national representation among the judges appointed in the courts, which is a serious risk for the legitimacy of both European courts.

The Dutch *Hoge Raad* takes another in-between position between the opposites of the *Cour de cassation* and the US Supreme Court. On the one hand, the institutional setting is copied from the French example, including the bifurcation between the official and the unofficial discourse. On the other hand, the *Hoge Raad* seeks legitimacy by improving the reasoning of the decisions, apparently aspiring to resemble the American courts. The resemblances and differences are illustrated by the way the different courts have dealt with wrongful life claims. As has been mentioned the rulings of the *Cour de cassation* and the California Supreme Court could not differ more in content and style. Again, the *Hoge Raad* takes the middle ground and draws from both institutional and discursive sources of legitimacy.

Finally, the question can be asked how to improve or strengthen the Courts' legitimacy? This review of the issues surrounding judicial legitimacy suggests that strengthening legitimacy will require improvement both in the input and output of the courts. On the input side, the possibility of political influence creates a serious reason about concern for the California Supreme Court (as well as the United States Supreme Court). For the *Cour de cassation* and the *Hoge Raad*, it is the elitist character of the court that attracts attention. The selection on merit creates risks for the representative nature of the courts and can be questioned from a democratic point of view. Though the weaknesses of the American and these European courts are mirror images of each other, they will both need to be aware of the risks they run on the input side. In addition, the *Cour de cassation* and (to a lesser extent) the *Hoge Raad* have to improve their performance on the output side. The example of the "wrongful life" cases shows that the *Hoge Raad* does reasonably well but could improve by introducing a practice of concurring and dissenting opinions. The *Cour de cassation* though has performed rather poorly in the cases of Nicolas Perruche and faces the risk of marginalization. For all courts discussed we can conclude that their legitimacy poses a serious challenge. In reflecting on this we should integrate the institutional, discursive and social dimensions of the problem. Only then can we aspire to improve the legitimacy of our courts.

The Autonomy of Defense and Defense Counsel

Philip Traest and Tessa Gombeer

The role of defense counsel during criminal proceedings is generally understood as being to provide legal assistance and personal support to clients and help in observing the rules of criminal procedure. Recently, however, safeguards of this legal assistance have been under increasing pressure. This raises the important question whether the true autonomy of defense counsel is being threatened by these developments.

International, European and Belgian legislative initiatives will be discussed in considering this question, but also the jurisprudence of the courts of Luxembourg (European Court of Justice) and Strasbourg (European Court of Human Rights). This discussion will offer an analysis of the norms relating to the independence of defense counsel that can be inferred from relevant case law.

1. RIGHTS OF THE DEFENSE AND RIGHT TO DEFENSE

International treaties, European documents and national criminal procedures contain a large catalogue of procedural safeguards, such as the right to silence, the right to examine witnesses and the right to not incriminate oneself. The right to legal assistance is the procedural precondition for an effective defense, and the basis of access to other procedural safeguards for defendants.[1]

1.1 United Nations: International Covenant on Civil and Political Rights

The International Covenant on Civil and Political Rights (ICCPR) provides procedural safeguards to individuals involved in criminal proceedings. It establishes the Human Rights Committee, which provides authoritative guidance on the right to a fair trial.

The rights granted under Article 14 of the Covenant are as follows. First, "All persons shall be equal before the courts and tribunals. In the determination of any criminal charge against him, or of his rights and obligations in a lawsuit, everyone shall be entitled to a fair and public hearing by a competent, independent and impartial tribunal established by law."[2] Publicity may sometimes be limited by the court, but only "to the extent strictly necessary in the opinion of the court in special circumstances where publicity would prejudice the interests of justice."[3]

The ICCPR also provides that, "any judgment rendered in a criminal case or in a lawsuit shall be made public, except where the interest of juvenile persons requires otherwise or the proceedings concern matrimonial disputes or the guardianship of children."[4] Everyone charged with a criminal offense shall have the right to be presumed innocent until proven guilty according to law.

---

[1] Taru Spronken, "'A place of greater safety.' Reflections on a European Charter for Criminal Defence Lawyers," 14, available at http://edata.ub.unimaas.nl/www-edocs/loader/file.asp?id=832.

[2] Article 14 International Covenant on Civil and Political Rights, adopted and opened for signature, ratification and accession by General Assembly resolution 2200 A (XXI) of 16 December 1966, http://www.unhchr.ch/html/menu3/b/a_ccpr.htm.

[3] *Id.*

[4] *Id.*

Article 14 of the Covenant adds that, in the determination of any criminal charge against him, everyone shall be entitled:

> to be tried in his presence, and to defend himself in person or through legal assistance of his own choosing; to be informed, if he does not have legal assistance, of this right; and to have legal assistance assigned to him, in any case where the interests of justice so require; and without payment by him in any such case if he does not have sufficient means to pay for it.[5]

In the case of juvenile persons, the procedure takes into account the delinquent's age and the desirability of promoting the delinquent's rehabilitation. Furthermore "[e]veryone convicted of a crime shall have the right to have his conviction and sentence reviewed by a higher tribunal according to law."[6] When by a final decision a person has been, convicted of a criminal offence and when subsequently his conviction has been reversed or he has been pardoned on the grounds that a new or newly discovered fact shows conclusively that there has been a miscarriage of justice, the person "shall be compensated according to the law, unless it is proven that the non-disclosure of the unknown fact in time is wholly or partly attributable to him."[7] Finally, "[n]o one shall be liable to be tried or punished again for an offence for which he has already been finally convicted or acquitted in accordance with the law and penal procedure of each country."[8]

---

[5] *Id.*

[6] *Id.*

[7] *Id.*

[8] *Id.*

1.2 Council of Europe: European Convention for the Protection of Human Rights and Fundamental Freedoms

The right to make a defense is at the core of the rights of the defendant, as laid down in, Article 6 of the European Convention for the Protection of Human Rights and Fundamental Freedoms.[9] Anyone charged with a criminal offence has a number of minimum rights, such as,

> to be informed promptly, in a language which he understands and in detail, of the nature and cause of the accusation against him, to have adequate time and the facilities for the preparation of his defense, to defend himself in person or through legal assistance of his own choosing, or, if he does not have sufficient means to pay for legal advice, to be given it free when the interests of justice so require, to examine or have examined witnesses against him and to obtain the attendance and examination of witnesses on his behalf under the same condition as witnesses against him and to have the free assistance of an interpreter if he cannot understand or speak the language used in court.[10]

Article 6, § 3 of the Convention contains an enumeration of specific applications of the general principle stated in paragraph 1 of the Article.[11] These principles are further developed in the case law of the European Court of Human

---

[9] Chris Van Den Wyngaert, *Kennismaking met de rechten van verdediging in strafzaken* (Antwerpen, Maklu, 2003), at 40.

[10] Article 6, § 3 European Convention for the Protection of Human Rights and Fundamental Freedoms, conventions.coe.int/Treaty/en/Treaties/Html/005.htm.

[11] Taru Spronken, *Verdediging. Een onderzoek naar de normering van het optreden van advocaten in strafzaken* (Deventer, Gouda Quint, 2001), at 439; Guy Stessens & Bart De Smet, "Artikel 6 § 3," in Johan Vande Lanotte & Yves Haeck (eds.), 1 *Handboek EVRM. Deel 2. Artikelsgewijze Commentaar* (Antwerpen, Intersentia, 2004), at 582.

Rights, as the Court recalls that the Convention is intended to guarantee rights that are practical and effective. "[T]his is in particular the case for the rights of the defense in view of the prominent place held in a democratic society by the right to a fair trial, from which they derive."[12]

The right to defense is as such absolute, but the rights of the defendant may be limited. The case law of the European Court of Human Rights indicates that the applicant does not have to prove that he has been aggrieved through the absence of the possibility to defend himself.[13] The importance of the right to legal assistance emerges from the provisional measure adopted in the context of the complaint against Turkey for the violation of Article 5 of the European Convention for the Protection of Human Rights and Fundamental Freedoms, with regard to the abduction and prosecution of Abdullah Öcalan. Öcalan's lawyers were not allowed access to their client, which resulted in the Court stating that Turkey should respect fully the rights of the defense and in particular the right of the applicant to see and have effective consultations in private with his lawyers.[14]

The specific rights mentioned in Article 6, § 3 of the European Convention for the Protection of Human Rights and Fundamental Freedoms are repeated in Article 14 of the International Covenant on Civil and Political Rights, Article 47 of the Charter of Fundamental Rights of the European Union and Article 8 of the American Convention on Human Rights.[15]

---

[12] European Court of Human Rights, 13 May 1980, Case of Artico v. Italy, No. 6694/74. The HUDOC Database is a information system which provides free online access to the case-law of the European Court of Human Rights. *See* http://www.echr.coe.int/ECHR/EN/Header/Case-Law/HUDOC/HUDOC+database/.

[13] *Id.*

[14] Taru Spronken, *supra* note 11, at 442.

[15] Bart De Smet, Jan Lathouwers, Karel Rimanque, Paul De Hert & Guy Stessens, "Artikel 6. Recht op een eerlijk proces," in Johan Vande Lanotte & Yves Haeck (eds.), 1 *Handboek EVRM. Deel 2. Artikelsgewijze Commentaar* (Antwerpen, Intersentia, 2004), at 386.

1.3 European Union

In 1997, the year in which the Amsterdam Treaty was signed, the European Union declared itself to be founded on respect for human rights and fundamental freedoms, principles that are common to the member states. Article 7 of the Treaty on European Union lays down strict rules concerning the sanctions for breaches of the obligation to respect these fundamental rights and freedoms, as guaranteed by the European Convention for the Protection of Human Rights and Fundamental Freedoms.[16]

1.3.1 Charter of Fundamental Rights

Since 2000, repressive measures in the context of the fight against (organized) crime within the European Union have been accompanied by measures concerning legal protection under the Charter of Fundamental Rights of the European Union. The Charter synthesizes the international obligations common to the member states and asserts that respect for the fundamental rights and freedoms of European citizens will be at the foundation of all European legislation. The rights are divided into six sections, entitled dignity, freedoms, equality, solidarity, citizen's rights and justice. The section entitled "justice" lays down the right to a fair trial and provides for the presumption of innocence, legality and proportionality of criminal offences and penalties and the extension of the principle of *ne bis in idem* to all the member states.[17] The Court of First Instance of the European Communities and various advocates general have declared the Charter nonbinding. Nevertheless, they recognize that it includes statements which appear in large measure to reaffirm rights

---

[16] Articles 6-7 Consolidated version Treaty on European Union, *O.J.* 24 December 2002, C 325/1.

[17] Articles 47-50 Charter of Fundamental Rights of the European Union, *O.J.* 18 December 2000, C 364/1.

enshrined in other instruments.[18]

Article 47 of the Charter of Fundamental Rights provides that "[e]veryone whose rights and freedoms guaranteed by the law of the Union are violated has the right to an effective remedy before a tribunal in compliance with the conditions laid down in this Article."[19] Everyone is furthermore, "entitled to a fair and public hearing within a reasonable time by an independent and impartial tribunal previously established by law. Everyone shall have the possibility of being advised, defended and represented. Legal aid shall be made available to those who lack sufficient resources in so far as such aid is necessary to ensure effective access to justice."[20]

1.3.2 Green Paper and Various Other Instruments Concerning Procedural Rights in Criminal Proceedings

In 2003, a Green Paper was published on procedural safeguards for suspects and defendants in criminal proceedings throughout the European Union. The Green Paper lays down five aspects of legal protection, comprising: the right to legal assistance and interpreters, the right to translation, the right to information of the accused, the protection of vulnerable groups and consular assistance.[21] Nevertheless, many states feel that there is no need for such minimum standards, since directions have been developed by the European Court of Human Rights.[22]

---

[18] *See for example*, Advocate general Tizzano in Court of Justice of the European Communities, Case C-173/99, The Queen v. Secretary of State for Trade and Industry *ex parte* BECTU, Rec. 2001, I-4881.

[19] Article 47 Charter of Fundamental Rights of the European Union, *O.J.* 18 December 2000, C 364/1.

[20] *Id.*

[21] Commission of the European Communities, COM (2003) 75 final, Brussels, 19 February 2003, Green paper from the Commission. Procedural Safeguards for Suspects and Defendants in Criminal Proceedings throughout the European Union.

[22] Taru Spronken, *supra* note 1, at 11-12.

The Green Paper provides that legal assistance and representation are the foundation of all other rights, for it is the duty of a criminal defense lawyer to make sure that the other fair trial rights of the alleged offender are respected. The Green Paper states that the right to legal assistance comes into operation upon arrest and that the alleged offender is entitled to legal assistance throughout the investigation and examination.[23] It fails to address this issue with respect to criminal cases that cross national borders.[24]

The European Parliament has adopted a Recommendation with a proposal for a European Parliament Recommendation to the Council on procedural safeguards for suspects and defendants in criminal proceedings throughout the European Union. It is striking that, as in the Green Paper, the Parliament states that the right to legal assistance must be complied with in each phase of the proceeding and that counsel should be able to assist clients during each interrogation.[25]

The Commission of the European Communities Proposal for a Council Framework Decision on certain procedural rights in criminal proceedings throughout the European Union lays down the right to legal advice, the obligation to provide for legal advice when certain circumstances arise, the obligation to ensure effectiveness of legal advice and the right to free legal advice. The right to legal advice is provided for the suspect as soon as possible and throughout the criminal proceedings, if he wishes to receive it. Moreover, a

---

[23] Commission of the European Communities, COM (2003) 75 final, Brussels, 19 February 2003, Green paper from the Commission. Procedural Safeguards for Suspects and Defendants in Criminal Proceedings throughout the European Union, introduction, §§ 2.5 and 4.

[24] Stellungnahme der Strafverteidigervereinigungen und der Arbeitsgruppe eu-defence zum Greenpaper from the Commission Procedural Safeguards for Suspects and Defendants in Criminal Proceedings throughout the European Union of 24 May 2003, available at http://www.organisation.strafverteidigervereinigungen.org.

[25] European Parliament, 2003/2179/INI, Brussels, 6 November 2003, European Parliament recommendation with a proposal for a European Parliament recommendation to the Council on procedural safeguards for suspects and defendants in criminal proceedings throughout the European Union, §§ 4, 7 and 19.

suspected person has the right to receive legal advice before answering questions in relation to the charge.[26] This is in line with the case law of the European Court of Human Rights, but is less far-reaching than the Parliament's Recommendation, and than the Green Paper, which states that the right to legal assistance arises immediately on arrest. The proposed Framework Decision also provides that member states must provide for a mechanism, which ensures the effectiveness of legal advice. The control mechanism must be put in place in a way that respects the independence of the defense.[27]

1.4 United States Constitution and American Convention on Human Rights

The Declaration of Independence of 1776 was itself a protest against the violation of rights by the government, and particularly against the abuse of criminal procedure to threaten life, liberty and the pursuit of happiness.[28] These ideas are further elaborated in the United States Bill of Rights, added to the American Constitution in 1791. The Sixth Amendment to the United States Constitution guarantees that in all criminal prosecutions the accused shall enjoy the right to have the assistance of counsel for his defense. In 1963 it was held that the right to counsel is constitutionally required in federal proceedings, and also in the several states, under the Due Process Clause of the Fourteenth Amendment. Every insolvent suspect has the right to free legal aid in

---

[26] COMMISSION OF THE EUROPEAN COMMUNITIES, COM (2004) 328 final, Brussels, 28 April 2004, Proposal for a Council Framework Decision on certain procedural rights in criminal proceedings throughout the European Union, Articles 2-5.

[27] Taru Spronken, "Ontwerp kaderbesluit procedurele rechten in strafzaken in de EU," *DD* (2004), at 986-87.

[28] P.J. Baauw, "Advocaat en mensenrechten. Strafrechtspleging en Straatsburg," *Advocatenblad* (1981), at 324.

felony cases[29] and in cases involving misdemeanors.[30] The influence of this due process revolution connects the right to defense to all the critical stages in the criminal proceedings, whenever substantial rights of the accused may be affected and the guiding hand of counsel is therefore necessary.[31] This is certainly the case for the first police interrogations after arrest, which is made clear by means of the *Miranda* warnings.[32] The influence of this due process revolution in Europe is found in the European Convention for the Protection of Human Rights and Fundamental Freedoms, at the level of the Council of Europe.[33]

The American Convention on Human Rights, that came into force on 18 July 1978, also protects the right to a fair trial:

> Every person has the right to a hearing, with due guarantees and within a reasonable time, by a competent, independent, and impartial tribunal, previously established by law, in the substantiation of any accusation of a criminal nature made against him or for the determination of his rights and obligations of a civil, labor, fiscal, or any other nature. Every person accused of a criminal offence has the right to be presumed innocent so long as his guilt has not been

---

[29] *See Gideon v. Wainwright*, 372 US 335 (1963).

[30] *See Argersinger v. Hamlin*, 407 US 25 (1972).

[31] P.J. Baauw, *supra* note 27, at 324.

[32] "The Constitution requires that I inform you of your rights. You have a right to remain silent. If you talk to any police officer, any thing you say can and will be used against you in court. You have a right to consult with a lawyer before you are questioned and may have him with you during questioning. If you wish to answer any questions, you have the right to stop answering at any time. You may stop answering at any time if you wish to talk to a lawyer and may have him with you during any further questioning." *Miranda v. Arizona*, 384 US 436 (1966).

[33] P.J. Baauw, *supra* note 27, at 325-326.

proven according to law.[34]

During these proceedings, the accused is entitled to:

> be assisted without charge by a translator or interpreter, if he does not understand or does not speak the language of the tribunal or court; prior notification in detail to the accused of the charges against him; adequate time and means for the preparation of his defense; the right of the accused to defend himself personally or to be assisted by legal counsel of his own choosing, and to communicate freely and privately with his counsel; the inalienable right to be assisted by counsel provided by the state, paid or not as the domestic law provides, if the accused does not defend himself personally or engage his own counsel within the time period established by law; the right of the defense to examine witnesses present in the court and to obtain the appearance, as witnesses, of experts or other persons who may throw light on the facts; the right not to be compelled to be a witness against himself or to plead guilty; and the right to appeal the judgment to a higher court. A confession of guilt by the accused shall be valid only if it is made without coercion of any kind. An accused person acquitted by a non-appealable judgment shall not be subjected to a new trial for the same cause. Criminal proceedings shall be public, except insofar as may be necessary to protect the interests of justice.[35]

With regard to the right to legal assistance, one must be aware that Article 8, § 2(c)-(e) of the American Convention also

---

[34] Article 8 American Convention on Human Rights, http://www.hrcr.org/docs/American_ Convention/oashr.html.

[35] *Id.*

declares the right to communicate freely and privately with his counsel, which differs from the European Convention on the Protection of Human Rights and Fundamental Freedoms. However, the European Commission of Human Rights and the European Court of Human Rights state that Article 6 of the European Convention on the Protection of Human Rights and Fundamental Freedoms must be read to include such a right.[36]

2. ACCESS TO LEGAL ASSISTANCE DURING PRELIMINARY PROCEEDINGS

The right to legal assistance concerns the right to counsel and the right to representation.[37] The moment at which the right to legal assistance becomes operative exposes the differences between Anglo-Saxon systems and continental systems. In Common Law countries, the right to legal assistance persists throughout police interrogation. In more inquisitorial systems, including Belgium, this right has not been acknowledged: the principle of free access overrides such a right. The reason for the denial of the right to legal assistance during police interrogation is the fear that the presence of counsel will negatively affect further investigation. Moreover, the Belgian legal system does not yet recognize the *cautio* obligation: police officers are not obliged to remind the accused of his right to silence. Of course, counsel, when present, would point out this right to their clients.[38]

---

[36] Taru Spronken, *supra* note 11, at 435, 469; Guy Stessens & Bart De Smet, *supra* note 11, at 601.

[37] European Court of Human Rights, April, 25 1983, Case of Pakelli v. Germany, No. 8398/78.

[38] Johannes A.W. Lensing, "De aanwezigheid van de raadsman bij het politieverhoor," *N.J.B.* (1982), at 1084-1085; Taru Spronken, *supra* note 1, at 21.

2.1 Council of Europe

2.1.1 Case Law of the European Court of Human Rights[39]

In the *Imbrioscia* case, the European Court of Human Rights held that the absence of counsel during the preliminary examination can harm the fairness of the trial as a whole, but the Court does not explicitly state that the alleged offender derives the right to legal assistance during such interrogations from Article 6 of the European Convention for the Protection of Human Rights and Fundamental Freedoms.[40] The *Murray* case points out that the refusal of access to counsel is a violation of Article 6 § 3(c) of the European Convention: a violation of the Convention was found because the accused was arrested for terrorist offences and refused access to a lawyer for 48 hours, notwithstanding the fact that the police pointed out in the beginning of the interrogation that invoking the right to silence could have negative consequences. Nevertheless, the right of legal assistance during police interrogations was not discussed: the Court merely pointed out that Murray should have been granted the opportunity to speak to his lawyer before the interrogation.[41] The *Murray* case thus endorses the *Imbrioscia* jurisprudence. The *Murray* jurisprudence was repeated in the *Averill*[42] and *Magee*[43] cases. The *Dikme* case then held that denial of access to a lawyer during the period

---

[39] *See* Franky Goossens, *Politiebevoegdheden en mensenrechten in Belgi. Een rechtsvergelijkend en internationaal onderzoek,* Dissertation, (Leuven, 2006), at 219-23

[40] European Court of Human Rights, 24 November 1993, Case of Imbrioscia v. Switzerland, No. 13972/88.

[41] European Court of Human Rights, 8 February 1996, Case of John Murray v. the United Kingdom, No. 18731/91.

[42] European Court of Human Rights, 6 June 2000, Case of Averill v. the United Kingdom, No. 36408/97: the European Court does not go into the complaint of Averill, with regard to the refusal of presence of counsel during police interrogations.

[43] European Court of Human Rights, 6 June 2000, Case of Magee v. the United Kingdom, No. 28135/95.

of police custody does not severely harm the fair character of the procedure as a whole, because national Turkish legislation did not associate a determining consequence to confessions obtained during police interrogations, when such confessions are disputed before the Court.[44]

In the *Can* case, the European Court of Human Rights stated that certain aspects of Article 6 § 3(c) of the European Convention for the Protection of Human Rights and Fundamental Freedoms are applicable during preliminary proceedings. The question whether legal assistance prevails during police interrogations was not answered.[45] Later, the European Court implicitly acknowledged the presence of the right to legal assistance during police questioning in Article 6 § 3(c) of the European convention in the *S* case. However, such a right was not considered to be absolute.[46]

In the *Dougan* case, the European Court of Human Rights stated that the alleged offender does not derive a right to legal assistance during police interrogations from Article 6 of the European Convention for the Protection of Human Rights and Fundamental Freedoms, except when there are exceptional circumstances.[47] This position was validated in the *Brennan* case,[48] but differentiated in the *Condron* case, in which the European Court stated that the presence of the lawyer involved is an important guarantee against self-incrimination.[49]

Access to a lawyer is generally discussed in the case of

---

[44] European Court of Human Rights, 11 July 2000, Case of Dikme v. Turkey, No. 20869/92.

[45] European Court of Human Rights, 30 September 1985, Case of Can v. Austria, No. 9300/81.

[46] European Court of Human Rights, 28 November 1991, Case of S v. Switzerland, No. 12629/87 and 13965/88.

[47] European Court of Human Rights, 14 December 1999, Case of Dougan, No. 44738/98.

[48] European Court of Human Rights, 16 October 2001, Case of Brennan v. the United Kingdom, No. 39846/98.

[49] European Court of Human Rights, 2 May 2000, Case of Condron v. the United Kingdom, No. 35718/97.

Öcalan, who was arrested on 15 February 2003, but denied access to his lawyers until 25 February 2003, a period during which he was interrogated on several occasions. In these circumstances, the Court held that to deny access to a lawyer for such a long period and in a situation where the rights of the defense might well be irretrievably prejudiced is detrimental to the rights of the defense to which the accused is entitled by virtue of Article 6 of the European Convention for the Protection of Human Rights and Fundamental Freedoms.[50]

Thus, the alleged offender does not derive a right to legal assistance during police interrogations from Article 6 of the European Convention for the Protection of Human Rights and Fundamental Freedoms. That proved to be a bridge too far.[51] Nevertheless, the European Court of Human Rights set out to ascertain whether the guarantees necessary to make the whole of the proceedings fair, including the preliminary proceedings, can give rise to the right to legal assistance in certain specific circumstances.[52] The right to legal assistance during police interrogations should be guaranteed in principle, because at this stage, the alleged offender is in need of information, advice and support.[53] Accordingly, the participation of the defense during preliminary proceedings is needed to guarantee the demand of the European Court of Human Rights that the defense must have rights which are practical and effective.[54] One can only hope that in the near future

---

[50] European Court of Human Rights, March 12, 2003, Case of Öcalan v. Turkey, No. 35718/97. The case was referred to the Grand Chamber, which delivered judgement on 5 May 2005.

[51] M.S. Groenhuijsen, "Het vooronderzoek in strafzaken. Algemeen deel," in M.S. Groenhuijsen & G. Knigge (eds.), *Vooronderzoek in strafzaken. Tweede interimrapport onderzoeksproject Strafvordering 2001* (Deventer, Gouda Quint, 2001), at 58; Taru Spronken, *supra* note 11, at 482.

[52] For example: European Court of Human Rights, 20 November 1989, Case of Kostovski v. the Netherlands, No. 11454/85 and European Court of Human Rights, 16 December 1992, Case of Edwards v. the United Kingdom, No. 13071/87.

[53] Taru Spronken, *supra* note 1, at 22.

[54] E. Prakken & Taru Spronken, "Grondslagen van het recht op verdediging," in C.H. Brants,

the European Court of Human Rights will join the European Commission, the European Committee for the Prevention of Torture and Inhuman or Degrading Treatment or Punishment and the Yugoslavia tribunal,[55] which acknowledges the right to legal assistance during interrogations in preliminary proceedings as an important human right.

2.1.2 Recommendations of the European Committee for the Prevention of Torture and Inhuman or Degrading Treatment or Punishment

The European Committee for the Prevention of Torture and Inhuman or Degrading Treatment or Punishment calls for the right to legal assistance during police interrogations. The Committee was set up under the 1987 Council of Europe Convention of the same name. The work of the Committee is designed to be an integrated part of the Council of Europe system for the protection of human rights, placing a proactive non-judicial mechanism alongside the existing reactive judicial mechanism of the European Court of Human Rights. The Committee focuses on Article 3 of the European Convention for the Protection of Human Rights and Fundamental Freedoms, concerning the prohibition of torture, inhumane or degrading treatment or punishment, whereas the European Court of Human Rights also considers Article 6 of the Convention. The Committee implements its essentially preventive function through periodic and *ad hoc* visits to places of detention.[56]

The Committee considers that access to a lawyer for persons in police custody should include the right to contact and to be visited by the lawyer (in both cases under conditions

---

P.A.M. Mevis & E. Prakken (eds.), *Legitieme strafvordering. Rechten van de mens als inspiratiebron in de 21ste eeuw* (Antwerpen, Intersentia, 2001), at 63.

[55] Yugoslavia tribunal, 2 September 1997, Case of Zdravko Mucic, No. IT-96-21-T, Trial chamber II.

[56] Council of Europe, The CPT in Brief, http://www.cpt.coe.int/en/about.htm.

guaranteeing the confidentiality of their discussions) as well as, in principle, the right for the person concerned to have the lawyer present during interrogation. However, in a number of countries there is considerable reluctance to comply with the Committee's Recommendation that the right of access to a lawyer be guaranteed from the very outset of custody. The Committee has repeatedly stressed that, in its experience, the period immediately following deprivation of liberty is when the risk of intimidation and physical ill treatment is greatest. Consequently, persons taken into police custody should have access to a lawyer during that period as a fundamental safeguard against ill treatment. The right of access to a lawyer must include the right to talk to him in private. The person concerned should also, in principle, be entitled to have a lawyer present during any interrogation conducted by the police. This should not prevent the police from questioning a detained person on urgent matters, even in the absence of a lawyer, nor rule out the replacement of a lawyer who impedes the proper conduct of an interrogation.[57]

A delegation of the Committee carried out a visit to Belgium from 18 April 2005 to 27 April 2005. It was the Committee's fourth periodic visit to Belgium. The Committee published the report on its visit to Belgium on 20 April 2006. The report emphasized that the majority of persons met by its delegation did not make allegations of ill treatment against the police. However, the lack of fundamental safeguards against ill treatment in police custody is still a cause for concern and the Committee has asked the Belgian authorities to give high priority to the adoption of relevant legislation, in particular, the right of access to a lawyer.[58]

---

[57] Council of Europe, The CPT Standards. The CPT's General Reports can be accessed at: http://www.cpt.coe.int

[58] Council of Europe, Rapport au Gouvernement de la Belgique relatif à la visite effectuée en Belgique par le Comité européen pour la prévention de la torture et des peines ou traitements inhumains ou dégradants (CPT) du 18 au 27 avril 2005, available at http://www.cpt.coe.int/documents/bel/2006-15-inf-fra.pdf.

2.2 European Union

In *Hoechst v. Commission*, the European Court of Justice held that the right to legal representation is one of the basic rights governing administrative procedure, the violation of which may lead to the imposition of penalties. The proceedings were not criminal, but the Court stated in a very broad way that, although certain rights of the defense relate only to the contentious proceedings which follow the delivery of the statement of objections, other rights, such as the right to legal representation, must be respected from the preliminary inquiry stage.[59]

At the European Union level, attention must also be paid to the Green Paper on procedural safeguards for suspects and defendants in criminal proceedings throughout the European Union, which provides that legal assistance and representation is the foundation of all other rights. The Green Paper states that the right to legal assistance comes into operation upon arrest and thus urges the importance of a right to the presence of counsel during police interrogations.[60]

2.3 Belgian Legal Procedure

Belgian legal procedure does not recognize a right to legal assistance during police interrogations, but it does not state the opposite either. Considering the circumstances, the police officer in charge of the interrogation may decide to allow the presence of counsel.[61]

---

[59] Court of Justice of the European Communities, Cases C-46/87 and C-227/88, Hoechst v. Commission, Rec. 1987, 1549, §§ 15-16. For cases of the Court of Justice of the European Communities, see http://www.curia.europa.eu.

[60] Commission of the European Communities, COM (2003) 75 final, Brussels, 19 February 2003, Green paper from the Commission. Procedural Safeguards for Suspects and Defendants in Criminal Proceedings throughout the European Union, introduction, §§ 2.5 and 4.

[61] Chris Van Den Wyngaert, *Strafrecht, Strafprocesrecht & Internationaal Strafrecht in hoofdlijnen. Deel II: Strafprocesrecht & internationaal strafrecht* (Antwerpen, Maklu, 2003),

3. AUTONOMY OF DEFENSE

Defense counsel may adduce all means deemed necessary to the defense: counsel is afforded much freedom to defend clients in the way they deem fit.[62] Counsel may for example appeal the limitation of the claim, even when this would result in the acquittal of a guilty client.[63] Reference can be made to international[64] and European regulations which protect lawyers against prosecution for activities undertaken in the legitimate defense of their clients.

3.1 Council of Europe: Recommendation (2000) 21 on the Freedom of Exercise of the Profession of Lawyer

Recommendation (2000) 21 of the Committee of Ministers to member states on the freedom of exercise of the profession of lawyer recommends that member states of the Council of Europe take any measure necessary to guarantee the freedom to practice the profession of lawyer, including the requirement that lawyers should not suffer or be threatened with any sanctions or pressure when acting in accordance with their professional standards. Lawyers should, however, respect the judiciary and carry out their duties toward the Court in a manner consistent with domestic legal and other

---

at 832.

[62] Taru Spronken, *supra* note 1, at 28.

[63] Koen Geens, "De advocaat: een onafhankelijke vriend," in X., *Liber Amicorum Jean-Pierre De Bandt* (Brussel, Bruylant, 2004), at 86.

[64] The UN basic principles on the role of lawyers, also referred to as the Havana principles, provide for an obligation of the authorities to safeguard the independence of lawyers. These principles state that lawyers must not fall victim to, not be threatened with, criminal prosecution or other sanctions, if they work in compliance with the standards and norms of conduct recognized by the profession. Lawyers must not be identified with their clients as a result of performing their professional duties and they should enjoy civil and penal immunity for relevant statements made in good faith in written or oral pleadings in their professional appearances before a court, tribunal or other legal or administrative authority. Basic Principles on the Role of Lawyers, adopted on 7 September 1990, http://www.unhchr.ch/html/menu3/b/h_comp44.htm.

rules, as well as in accordance with professional standards.[65]

3.2 Council of Europe: Case Law of the European Court of Human Rights

Article 10 of the European Convention for the Protection of Human Rights and Fundamental Freedoms protects freedom of expression. In its second paragraph it specifies that the exercise of that freedom carries duties and responsibilities and may be subject to limitations, if they are "prescribed by law, and necessary in a democratic society," in order to meet certain objectives, such as the protection of the reputation or rights of others and maintaining the authority and impartiality of the judiciary.[66] Defense counsel may not undermine judicial authority, but the case law of the European Court of Human Rights shows that submissions of counsel confined to the courtroom, will not be viewed in as negative a light as criticisms voiced in the media.[67]

Mr Schöpfer, a lawyer, complained publicly about criminal proceedings which were at that time pending before a criminal court. The Court considered that:

> it is true that Article 10 of the European Convention for the Protection of Human Rights and Fundamental Freedoms protects not only the substance of the ideas and information expressed, but also the form in

---

[65] Recommendation Rec (2000) 21 of the Committee of Ministers to member states on the freedom of exercise of the profession of lawyer, adopted by the Committee of Ministers on 25 October 2000, I.4 and III.4. *See* https://wcd.coe.int/com.instranet.InstraServlet?Command=com.instranet.CmdBlobGet&DocId=370284&SecMode=1&Admin=0&Usage=4&InstranetImage=62250.

[66] Article 10 European Convention for the Protection of Human Rights and Fundamental Freedoms, available at http://conventions.coe.int/Treaty/en/Treaties/Html/005.htm.

[67] Dirk Voorhoof, "Straatsburg waakt over de expressievrijheid van advocaten," *Juristenkrant* (2002), at 7.

which they are conveyed. It also goes without saying that freedom of expression is secured to lawyers too, who are certainly entitled to comment in public on the administration of justice, but their criticism must not overstep certain bounds. In that connection, account must be taken of the need to strike the right balance between the various interests involved, which include the public's right to receive information about questions arising from judicial decisions, the requirements of the proper administration of justice, and the dignity of the legal profession. Because of their direct, continuous contact with their members, the Bar authorities and a country's courts are in a better position than an international court to determine how, at a given time, the right balance can be struck. That is why they have a certain margin of appreciation in assessing the necessity of interference in this area, but this margin is subject to European supervision.... In addition to the general nature, the seriousness and the tone of the applicant's assertions, the Court notes that the applicant first held a press conference, claiming that this was his last resort, and only afterwards lodged an appeal before the Lucerne Court of Appeal, which was partly successful. He also omitted to apply to the other supervisory body for the district authority, the public prosecutor's office, whose ineffectiveness he did not attempt to establish except by means of mere assertions. Having regard also to the modest amount of the fine imposed on the applicant, the Court considers that the authorities did not go beyond their margin of appreciation in punishing Mr Schöpfer.[68]

Accordingly there was no breach of Article 10 of the Conven-

---

[68] European Court of Human Rights, 20 May 1998, Case of Schöpfer v. Switzerland, No. 25405/94.

tion. The *Schöpfer* case shows that freedom of expression may be restricted in view of the special position of lawyers in the administration of justice.[69]

In the *Nikula* case, "the applicant alleged that her freedom of expression had been infringed on account of her having been convicted of public defamation for having criticised, in her capacity as defence counsel, the public prosecutor's decisions to press charges against a certain person."[70] It is striking that the European Court of Human Rights refered to a survey with regard to a number of member states of the Council of Europe and of certain other countries. A great majority of such countries provide a privilege for lawyers for statements they make while representing clients in court. Every surveyed state recognized that "a lawyer's ability to express himself or herself is closely linked to counsel's obligation to defend the client."[71] To the extent that restrictions are permitted on a lawyer's statements in court, most of the jurisdictions surveyed tended to favor the use of disciplinary measures over criminal sanctions. In most of the jurisdictions surveyed, criminal sanctions were rarely used in practice, and then usually only in extreme circumstances and provided that intent could be shown, as opposed to mere negligence. Even where a lawyer's statements may in principle be subject to restrictions, those restrictions are generally imposed only when the statement is not only defamatory but also entirely unrelated to the proceedings or the parties. Almost all of the jurisdictions surveyed recognized the fundamental difference between the roles of the prosecutor, who is the opponent of the accused, and the judge, who is not. This distinction generally provides an increased protection for

---

[69] Dirk Voorhoof, *supra* note 67, at 1.

[70] European Court of Human Rights, 21 March 2002, Case of Nikula v. Finland, No. 31611/96

[71] *Id.*

statements that are critical of the prosecutor.[72]

The European Court of Human Rights stressed "the duty of the courts and the presiding judge to direct proceedings in such a manner as to ensure the proper conduct of the parties and above all the fairness of the trial – rather than to examine in a subsequent trial the appropriateness of a party's statements in the courtroom."[73] The court considered that:

> the threat of an ex post facto review of counsel's criticism of another party to criminal proceedings – which the public prosecutor doubtlessly must be considered to be – is difficult to reconcile with defense counsel's duty to defend their clients' interests zealously. It follows that it should be primarily for counsel themselves, subject to supervision by the bench, to assess the relevance and usefulness of a defense argument without being influenced by the potential "chilling effect" of even a relatively light criminal sanction or an obligation to pay compensation for harm suffered or costs incurred.[74]

It is therefore only in exceptional cases that restriction of defense counsel's freedom of expression can be accepted as necessary in a democratic society. In the court's view, "such reasons have not been shown to exist and the restriction on Ms Nikula's freedom of expression therefore failed to answer any 'pressing social need'."[75] The Court thus concluded that Article 10 of the European Convention for the Protection of Human Rights and Fundamental Freedoms was violated.[76]

---

[72] *Id.*

[73] *Id.*

[74] *Id.*

[75] *Id.*

[76] *Id.*; The judgment is discussed by Dirk Voorhoof, *supra* note 67, at 1, 7; W. Van Gerven,

In the *Nikula* case, the Court does not exclude the possibility that, in certain circumstances, interference with counsel's freedom of expression in the course of the trial could also raise an issue under Article 6 of the European Convention for the Protection of Human Rights and Fundamental Freedoms with regard to the right of the accused to receive a fair trial. "'Equality of arms' and other considerations of fairness are therefore in favor of free and even forceful exchange of argument between the parties."[77]

The case law of the European Court of Human Rights makes a distinction between submissions of counsel confined to the courtroom and criticism against a judge or a prosecutor expressed in the media. With regard to submissions of counsel confined to the court, the Court holds that it is primarily up to counsel itself to decide what is appropriate to say, to avoid the "chilling effect" of possible penalties. As to criticism voiced in the media, it seems that criticism concerning an important social debate can rely on the protection that the Court normally gives to opinions and information that concern the *res publica*, to preserve an open discussion of matters of public concern.[78]

In the *Kyprianou* case, the complaints of the applicant, an advocate, originated in his conviction for contempt of court. The applicant was defending someone accused of murder before the Limassol Assize Court. He was conducting the cross-examination of a prosecution witness, a police officer, and alleged that the court interrupted him after he had put a question to the witness. He claimed that he felt offended and had sought permission to withdraw from the case. The government asserted that the court made a routine intervention with a simple and polite remark regarding the manner

---

"Pleidooi voor een beleid van de advocatuur," *NjW* (2002), at 9, 12.

[77] European Court of Human Rights, 21 March 2002, Case of Nikula v. Finland, No. 31611/96.

[78] Dirk Voorhoof, *supra* note 67, at 7; Dirk Lindemans, "De vrijheid van meningsuiting van de advocaat en art. 444 Ger. W.," *P.&B.* (2004), at 16.

in which the applicant was cross-examining the witness. The applicant, however, immediately interrupted, without allowing the court to finish its remark and refused to proceed with his cross-examination.

After a short break the Assize Court, by a majority, sentenced the applicant to five days' imprisonment and imposed a fine. The applicant argued that a sanction for contempt of court should not be used to suppress aggressive advocacy, because the advocate should have sufficient freedom to conduct his client's case as he sees fit. The applicant further contended that he had not been heard by an independent and impartial tribunal, that he had been presumed guilty as soon as he objected to the Assize Court's conduct and that the Assize Court failed to inform him in detail of the accusations against him. Finally, the applicant complained of interference with his right to freedom of expression, which was not prescribed by law, and that the imposition of a fine and a prison term were disproportionate to any governmental objective. The European Court of Human Rights considered that the essential issues raised by the applicant were considered under Article 6 of the European Convention for the Protection of Human Rights and Fundamental Freedoms and held that there was a violation of Article 6 §§ 2, 3 and 3(a) of the Convention. Accordingly, the Court did not consider it necessary to examine separately whether Article 10 was also violated. The Grand Chamber held that it is not necessary to examine the complaint separately under Article 6, §§ 2 and 3(a) of the Convention when a violation of § 1 has been stated. The Grand Chamber also upheld violation of Article 10 of the Convention.[79]

---

[79] European Court of Human Rights, 15 December 2005, Case of Kyprianou v. Cyprus, No. 73797/01.

4. AUTONOMY OF DEFENSE COUNSEL

4.1 Conception of the Role of Defense Counsel

The specific role of counsel has been stated by the European Court of Human Rights: regarding the key role of lawyers in this field, it is legitimate to expect defense counsel to contribute to the proper administration of justice, and thus to help to maintain public confidence in the courts.[80] The Court of First Instance of the European Communities has also held that lawyers are expected to contribute to the proper administration of the judicial machinery: "the requirement to have recourse to a third party is based on a conception of the lawyers' role as collaborating in the administration of justice and as being required to provide, in full independence and in the overriding interests of justice, such legal assistance as his client needs."[81] Such a conception reflects legal traditions common to member states and is also to be found in Article 17 of the EC Statute.[82]

Perceptions of the duties of defense counsel are closely related to the criminal procedures within which criminal defense lawyers operate. Proceedings in common law countries are of a more accusatorial nature in comparison with civil law countries, where proceedings are more inquisitorial. Each country has its own perception of professional practice.[83] Nevertheless, the core duty of the criminal defense lawyer is to safeguard the ability of the accused to defend

---

[80] European Court of Human Rights, 20 May 1998, Case of Schöpfer v. Switzerland, No. 25405/94; European Court of Human Rights, 21 March 2002, Case of Nikula v. Finland, No. 31611/96.

[81] Court of First Instance of the European Communities, Case T-79/99, Euro-Lex v. OHMI (EU-Lex), Rec. 1999, II-3555.

[82] *Id. See also* Court of Justice of the European Communities, Case C-155/79, AM & S v. Commission, Rec. 1982, 1616.

[83] Taru Spronken, *supra* note 1, at 3.

himself.[84]   The three core assumptions in this respect are partiality, independence and confidentiality.[85]

The Court of Justice of the European Communities has held that it is the duty of defense counsel to act for their clients in complete independence and in the client's sole interest, to avoid all risk of conflict and to observe strict professional secrecy.[86] The Court of Justice does not define these concepts, but the opinion of Advocate-general Léger offers insight: independence requires lawyers to carry out their advisory duties and those of assistance and representation in the client's exclusive interest. Independence must be demonstrated *vis-à-vis* the public authorities, other operators and third parties, by whom they may never be influenced. Independence must also be demonstrated *vis-à-vis* the client, who may not become his lawyer's employer. Independence is an essential guarantee for the individual and for the judiciary, with the result that lawyers are obliged not to get involved in business or joint activities which threaten to compromise it. Professional secrecy forms the basis of the relationship of trust between lawyer and client. It requires the lawyer not to divulge any information imparted by the client, and extends *ratione temporis* to the period after the lawyer has ceased to act for the client and *ratione personae* to third parties. Professional secrecy also constitutes an essential guarantee of the freedom of the individual and of the proper working of justice, so that in most member states it is a matter of public policy. Lastly, lawyers owe a duty of loyalty to their clients, which requires them to avoid conflicts of interest. That duty means that a lawyer may not advise, assist or represent parties

---

[84] *See* European Court of Human Rights, 30 September 1985, Case of Can v. Austria, No. 9300/81.

[85] Hugo Lamon, *Een advocaat in de Spiegel. Beschouwingen over balie en advocatuur* (Brugge, die Keure, 2004), at 16; Taru Spronken, *supra* note 1, at 18.

[86] Court of Justice of the European Communities, Case C-309/99, Wouters v. Nova, Rec. 2002, I-2289.

whose interests are, or in the past were, opposed. In addition, lawyers may not use to the benefit of one client information concerning, or obtained from, another client.[87]

4.2 Independence as Core Assumption

Independence is a condition which has several connotations. The responsibilities of defense counsel call for an independent attitude toward the authorities, their clients and other parties involved. The independence of the criminal defense lawyer serves to guarantee partiality: counsel must be guided by the best interests and the wishes of their clients, even when such interests conflict with the interests of the authorities.[88] Counsel may use the law in a strategic way,[89] knowing that they may never breach their independence.[90]

4.2.1 Independence of Defense Counsel in Relation to the Client
4.2.1.1 Defense of the Interests of the Client
Defense counsel has professional knowledge of criminal proceedings, which should be used to make a realistic and effective assessment of the possible defense strategies. Nevertheless, the defense of the interests of the client may not be contrary to the law. There is a strong similarity between steps that may be taken in defense of a client's interests by defense counsel and the principles of proportionality and subsidiarity, which guarantee the interest of good practice.[91]

---

[87] Opinion Advocate General Léger, delivered on 10 July 2001, Case C-309/99, Wouters/Nova, 19 February 2002.

[88] Hugo Lamon, "De blinde rechter en de dove advocaat. De verhoudingen tussen balie en magistratuur in de 21ste eeuw," *NjW* (2003), at 1102; Taru Spronken, *supra* note 1, at 19.

[89] Marc A. Loth, "De publieke verantwoordelijkheid van de advocatuur," *Advocatenblad* (2003), at 28.

[90] Hugo Lamon, *supra* note 88, at 1102.

[91] Taru Spronken, *supra* note 1, at 19.

The preamble to the Code of Conduct for lawyers in the European Union lays down that a lawyer must serve the interests of justice as well as those whose rights and liberties he is trusted to assert and defend, and his duty is not only to plead his client's cause but to be his adviser. A lawyer's function therefore gives rise to a variety of legal and moral obligations.[92] Two different conceptions of "the interests of justice" must be distinguished. The first equates the interests of justice with the interests of combating crime. The second takes the interests of justice to be synonymous with the protection of fundamental human rights, within the limits of the law, and if necessary against the interests of law enforcement.[93]

4.2.1.2 Defense Counsel Regarded as the Extension of Their Criminal Clients

In some instances powers are exclusively granted to counsel. This legal fiction means that the rights of the alleged offender are respected when counsel exercises these powers.[94] This is supported by the case law of the European Court of Human Rights with regard to adversary treatment. In the *Doorson* case the European Court accepted the system of indirect confrontation in front of the examining magistrate, in which the counsel alone is present at the hearing and has the opportunity to question the witness. The Court did recall that even when these counterbalancing procedures are found to compensate sufficiently for the handicaps under which the defense labors, a conviction should not be based solely or to a decisive extent on anonymous statements.[95]

---

[92] Preamble to the Code of Conduct for Lawyers in the European Union, available at http://www. ccbe.org/doc/En/code2002_en.pdf#search=%22code%20of%20conduct%20for%20lawyers%2 0in%20the%20European%20Union%22.

[93] Taru Spronken, *supra* note 1, at 20.

[94] *Id.* at 23-24.

[95] European Court of Human Rights, 26 March 1996, Case of Doorson v. the Netherlands, No. 20524/92; European Court of Human Rights, 14 February 2002, Case of Visser v. the

This case law can put great strain on the relationship between counsel and clients. Counsel, present during the interrogation can, for example, learn the identity of the witness, but counsel may not disclose the identity of the witnesses identity to their clients.[96]

The Belgian legal provisions concerning anonymous witnesses provide that the interrogation will be managed by the examining magistrate. Counsel and their clients (persons against whom criminal proceedings are started, accused suspects and civil parties) are allowed to be present during the interrogation of the completely anonymous witness, without having the ability to pose questions to the witness. When concealing the identity of the witness is warranted, counsel and their clients will attend the interrogation in a separate room from the examining judge and the witness. Nevertheless, counsel has the possibility of posing (oral or written) questions prior to or during the interrogation. The examining magistrate himself judges the utility of the questions posed.[97] Belgian legislation does not violate the European Convention for the Protection of Human Rights and Fundamental Freedoms, because case law holds that it is sufficient that counsel or their clients are present during the interrogation and have the opportunity to pose additional questions.[98]

The European Court of Human Rights looks upon respect for the rights of the defense from the perspective of the defense as a whole, *i.e.*, it tests whether these rights could be asserted, regardless of the answer to the question: who exercised the

---

Netherlands, No. 2668/95; European Court of Human Rights, 28 March 2002, Case of Birutis and others v. Lithuania, No. 47698/99 and 48115/99.

[96] Alain De Nauw, "De wet op de anonimiteit van getuigen," *R.W.* (2002-2003), at 928; Frank Schuermans, *Anonieme getuige. Een eerste commentaar op de Wet van 8 april 2002 betreffende de anonimiteit van de getuigen* (Brussel, De Boeck & Larcier, 2003), at 48.

[97] *See* Article 86 ter Belgian Code of Criminal Procedure.

[98] Alain De Nauw, *supra* note 96, at 925.

rights in question? The specific factual circumstances of the involved case are of great importance.[99] Nevertheless, the attribution of more powers to counsel than to the alleged offender results in the restriction of the rights of the defendant: exercise of the powers by the lawyer is translated into respect for the rights of the defendant. This can have serious negative consequences for the relationship between counsel and their clients, which should be based on trust.[100]

4.2.2 Independence of Defense Counsel in Relation to the Authorities

4.2.2.1 Principle of Professional Confidentiality

Professional privilege assures that what comes to the knowledge of counsel within the context of legal assistance remains confidential.[101] The professional confidentiality of the criminal defense lawyer is a condition *sine qua non* for the functioning of the relationship between defense counsel and their clients.[102] Professional confidentiality also implies that the parties involved are free to discontinue their relationship when an irretrievable breach of trust has taken place.[103]

Professional confidentiality guarantees that counsel cannot be forced to reveal confidential information as a witness. Moreover, this professional privilege implies that measures should be taken to prevent confidential communications from being disclosed through investigative methods, such as telephone conversation intercepts.[104]

---

[99] E. Prakken & Taru Spronken, *supra* note 54, at 67; Taru Spronken, *supra* note 11, at 459-463.

[100] E. Prakken & Taru Spronken, *supra* note 54, at 71.

[101] Pierre Lambert, *Le Secret Professionnel* (Brussel, Nemesis, 1985), at 115. In Belgium the violation of the obligation of secrecy is punished through means of criminal sanctions, in Article 458 of the Belgian Penal Code.

[102] Hugo Lamon, *supra* note 88, at 1105.

[103] Taru Spronken, *surpa* note 1, at 20.

[104] *Id.*

4.2.2.2 Professional Confidentiality Under Threat

Without the independence of the criminal defense lawyer, there can be no effective defense. However, international, European and Belgian legislators have begun to weaken the defense counsel's independence, by subordinating this independence to the interests of the investigation.

4.2.2.2.1 Fight Against Organized Crime

In the last decade, an extensive international and regional legal framework was developed for combating organized crime. Various cooperation levels deal with organized crime issues with relevance for the European Union, such as the Group of Eight (G8), the Organization for Economic Cooperation and Development, the United Nations and the Council of Europe. The most important legal instruments for combating organized crime have been developed at the level of the United Nations and the European Union.[105]

4.2.2.2.2 United Nations: Convention against Transnational Organized Crime

The United Nations has a crucial role to play in the struggle against organized crime. The Convention against Transnational Organized Crime is the first legally binding United Nations instrument in the area of organized crime, which came into force on 29 September 2003. Belgium and the United States both signed and ratified the Convention. The Convention requires states that are parties to criminalize participation in an organized criminal group; money laundering, including the laundering of the proceeds of crime; corruption; and obstruction of justice. Not only natural persons, but also legal persons, can be held liable for taking part in or profiting from serious crimes involving an organized criminal group or for money-laundering activities.[106]

---

[105] *See* Gert Vermeulen & Tom Vander Beken, "International/regional legal framework for combating organized crime," in Brice De Ruyver, Gert Vermeulen & Tom Vander Beken (eds.), *Strategies for the EU and the US in Combating Transnational Organized Crime* (Antwerpen, Maklu, 2002), at 201-25.

[106] Articles 5-6, 8, 10 and 23 of the United Nations Convention against Transnational Organized

According to Article 5 of the Convention against Transnational Organized Crime, each party shall adopt such (legal) measures as

> may be necessary to establish as criminal offences, when committed intentionally (i) Agreeing with one or more other persons to commit a serious crime for a purpose relating directly or indirectly to the obtaining of a financial or other material benefit and, where required by domestic law, involving an act undertaken by one of the participants in furtherance of the agreement or involving an organized criminal group[107] (ii) Conduct by a person who, with knowledge of either the aim and general criminal activity of an organized criminal group or its intention to commit the crimes in question, takes an active part in: a. Criminal activities of the group; b. Other activities of an organized criminal group in the knowledge that his or her participation will contribute to the achievement of the criminal aim.[108]

According to Article 5 of the Convention, organizing, directing, aiding, abetting, facilitating, or counseling serious crimes involving organized criminal groups must also be made criminal offences.[109]

Article 6 of the Convention against Transnational Organ-

Crime, adopted and opened for signature, ratification and accession by General Assembly resolution A/RES/55/25 of 15 November 2000, http://www.unodc.org/pdf/crime/a_res_55/res5525e.pdf.

[107] United Nations Convention against Transnational Organized Crime Art. 2(a) ("'Organized criminal group' shall mean a structured group of three or more persons, existing for a period of time and acting in concert with the aim of committing one or more serious crimes or offences established in accordance with the convention in order to obtain, directly or indirectly, a financial or other material benefit").

[108] *Id.* Article 5.

[109] *Id.*

ized Crime states that activities relating to money laundering must be criminalized. This extends to cash as well as to any form of property which is the proceeds of crime, and includes any form of transfer or conversion of the property for the purpose of concealing its true origin. Simple acquisition or possession is also included if the person in possession knows that the property is the proceeds of crime.[110]

The Convention establishes important rules with regard to the jurisdiction over the four specific crimes, acknowledges the importance of international cooperation and takes into account the protection of victims and witnesses. All states that ratify the Convention must commit themselves to prevent organized crime as much as possible, for example, by promoting codes of conduct for relevant professions, in particular, lawyers, notaries public, tax consultants and accountants.[111]

(a) European Union

At the European Union level, Article 29 of the Treaty on European Union provides that the area of freedom, security and justice shall be achieved by preventing and combating racism, xenophobia and (organized) crime.[112] This idea has been elaborated in various policy documents, such as the Vienna Action Plan,[113] the Tampere Presidency Conclusions[114] and the Millennium Strategy, as well as various legal instruments.

---

[110] *Id.* Article 6. Article 7 of the Convention obliges states parties to take measures to combat money laundering.

[111] *Id.* Articles 15, 16-22, 24-25, 31.

[112] Article 29 Consolidated version Treaty on European Union, *O.J.* 24 December 2002, C 325/1.

[113] Action Plan of the Council and the Commission on How to Best Implement the Provisions of the Treaty of Amsterdam on an Area of Freedom, Security and Justice, *O.J.* 23 January 1999, C 19/1.

[114] Tampere Presidency Conclusions, 15 October 1999–16 October 1999, http://www.presidency.finland.fi/frame.asp.

The Millennium Strategy, the follow-up to the 1997 Action Plan to combat organized crime, sets the goals to be achieved in the fight against organized crime in the years to come. The strategy encourages the approximation of criminal law in certain areas, including financial crime, especially money laundering.[115]

The European Union has also addressed the organized crime problem. The Action Plan of 28 April 1997 to combat organized crime considers the problem of organized crime.[116] On 21 December 1998 the Council adopted Joint Action 98/733/JHA on making it a criminal offence to participate in a criminal organization in the member states of the European Union.[117] Mention also has to be made of the Resolution of 21 December 1998 on the prevention of organized crime with reference to the establishment of a comprehensive strategy for combating it.[118] There is now a proposal for a Framework Decision in combating organized crime. Certain acts of participation in a criminal organized group, defined in the United Nations Convention against Transnational Organized Crime, but not explicitly mentioned in the Joint Action of 1998, are made criminal offences in Article 2 of the proposed Framework Decision.[119]

(b) Belgian Penal Code

Article 324 ter, § 2 of the Belgian penal code makes the participation in the preparation or execution of any lawful

---

[115] The prevention and control of organised crime. A European Union Strategy for the beginning of the new Millennium, *O.J.* 3 March 2000, C 124/1.

[116] Action plan of 28 April 1997 to combat organized crime, *O.J.* 15 August 1997, C 251/1.

[117] Joint action of 21 December 1998 adopted by the Council on the basis of Article K.3 of the Treaty on European Union, on making it a criminal offence to participate in a criminal organisation in the Member States of the European Union, *O.J.* 29 December 1998, L 351/1.

[118] Council Resolution of 21 December 1998 on the prevention of organised crime with reference to the establishment of a comprehensive strategy for combating it, *O.J.* 29 December 1998, C 408/1.

[119] Commission of the European Communities, COM (2005) 6 def., Brussels, 19 January 2005, Proposal of Framework Council Decision on the fight against organised crime.

act of an organized criminal group,[120] with knowledge of the fact that his or her participation will contribute to the aim of the organized group, a criminal offence.[121] A lawyer who defends a criminal organization before a Belgian court or tribunal cannot be prosecuted as such. But the question arises whether this is also true when counsel, through its defense, ensures the continuation of the activities of the criminal organization.[122] The Belgian legislation is not very clear as to what extent counsel can be prosecuted for participation in the activities of a criminal organization: the vague phrasing of the legal provision goes beyond the precise wording of the United Nations Convention against Transnational Organized Crime. The question has thus to be posed whether the abstract wording of the crime "participation in a criminal organization" in the Belgian legislation is compatible with the principle of the independence of Belgian criminal defense lawyers.

4.2.2.2.3 *Fight Against Money Laundering*
4.2.2.2.3.1 *Preventive Component*
(a) European Union

Council Directive 91/308/EEC of 10 June 1991 on prevention of the use of the financial system for the purpose of money laundering has been updated by means of a second directive, Directive 2001/97/EC of the European Parliament and of the Council of 4 December 2001. This requires the member states of the European Union to bring such laws, regulations and other administrative provisions into force as are necessary to comply with the second Directive, which amends the first Directive of 1991, by 15 June 2003. The

---

[120] Article 324 bis Belgian Penal Code (organised criminal group is defined as a structured group of more than two persons, existing for a period of time and acting in concert with the aim of committing one or more serious crimes or offences in order to obtain, directly or indirectly, a material benefit).

[121] Article 324 ter, § 2 Belgian Penal Code.

[122] *Parl. St.* Senaat 1997-1998, nr. 1-662/4.

member states are prompted to subject independent legal professionals (*i.e.*, lawyers) to the obligation of reporting suspicious transactions.[123] This obligation is a far-reaching restriction on the professional secrecy of counsel.

Article 12 of the first Directive stated that the member states shall ensure that the provisions of the Directive are extended in whole or in part to professions or other categories of undertakings, other than the credit and financial institutions, which engage in activities which are particularly likely to be used for money-laundering purposes.[124] The second directive holds that lawyers have an obligation of reporting suspicious transactions in two circumstances. First, lawyers must report when they assist in the planning or execution of transactions for their clients concerning the buying and selling of real property or business entities; the management of client money, securities and other assets; the opening or management of bank, savings or securities accounts; the organization of contributions necessary for the creation, operation or management of companies; or the creation, operation or management of trusts, companies or similar structures.

They also have this obligation when acting on behalf of and for their client in any financial or real estate transaction. However, when lawyers provide legal advice, ascertaining the legal position of a client or representing a client in legal proceedings, it would not be appropriate to put them under the obligation to report information obtained before, during or after judicial proceedings, or in the course of ascertaining the legal position of the client. Therefore, member states are

---

[123] Article 3 Directive 2001/97/EC of the European Parliament and of the Council of 4 December 2001 amending Council Directive 91/308/EEC on prevention of the use of the financial system for the purpose of money laundering, *O.J.* 28 December 2001, L 344/76.

[124] Article 12 Council Directive 91/308/EEC of 10 June 1991 on prevention of the use of the financial system for the purpose of money laundering, *O.J.* 28 June 1991, L 166/77.

not obliged to apply the obligation in these circumstances.[125] *De facto*, it is not easy to distinguish between assisting in the planning of transactions for clients and providing legal advice ascertaining the legal position of clients.[126] Nevertheless, legal advice remains subject to the obligation of professional secrecy unless the legal counselor is taking part in money laundering activities, the legal advice is provided for money laundering purposes, or the lawyer knows that the client is seeking legal advice for money laundering purposes.[127]

Member states may designate an appropriate self-regulatory body of the legal profession to be informed of facts which might be an indication of money laundering. This option is designed to take proper account of counsel's duty of discretion owed to clients. Disclosure in good faith to the authorities responsible for combating money laundering by an institution or person subject to this Directive shall not constitute a breach of any restriction on disclosure of information imposed by contract or by any legislative, regulatory or administrative provision.[128]

---

[125] Preamble, § 17 and Articles 1.2, 1.5 Directive 2001/97/EC of the European Parliament and of the Council of 4 December 2001 amending Council Directive 91/308/EEC on prevention of the use of the financial system for the purpose of money laundering, *O.J.* 28 December 2001, L 344/76 *iuncto* Article 2a.5 and 6, 1° and 3° Council Directive 91/308/EEC of 10 June 1991 on prevention of the use of the financial system for the purpose of money laundering, *O.J.* 28 June 1991, L 166/77

[126] Philip Traest, "Advocaten weldra onderworpen aan de meldingsplicht inzake witwassen: spanning tussen overheidsbeleid en een onafhankelijke advocatuur," in X., *Liber Amicorum Jean-Pierre De Bandt* (Brussel, Bruylant 2004), at 219.

[127] Preamble, § 17 and Articles 1.2 and 1.5 Directive 2001/97/EC of the European Parliament and of the Council of December 4, 2001 amending Council Directive 91/308/EEC on prevention of the use of the financial system for the purpose of money laundering, *O.J.* December 28, 2001, L 344/76.

[128] Preamble, § 20 and Articles 1.5, 1.9 Directive 2001/97/EC of the European Parliament and of the Council of 4 December 2001 amending Council Directive 91/308/EEC on prevention of the use of the financial system for the purpose of money laundering iuncto art. 6, 3° and 9 Council Directive 91/308/EEC of 10 June 1991 on prevention of the use of the financial system for the purpose of money laundering, *O.J.* 28 June 1991, L 166/77.

(b) Belgian Regulation

The provisions of the money laundering Directives are implemented by means of the law of 11 January 1993 to prevent using the financial system for money laundering, which has been reviewed on several occasions.[129] The obligation of reporting breaches the relationship based on trust between counsel and their clients.[130] Moreover, the right to defense is threatened because the clients will feel inhibited from giving their counsel all the information needed for their defense. The relationship between counsel and the public prosecutor will become more problematic as a result of the obligation of reporting, because this obligation involves defense counsel, to some degree in the prosecution of criminal offences.[131]

The second money laundering Directive does not detract as much from counsel's professional secrecy, since the pressure put on the confidentiality of lawyers[132] is interconnected with the definition of the criminal offence regarding money laundering.[133] The European Union member states can decide to go beyond the rules of the directive.

4.2.2.2.3.2 Repressive Component

The suppression of money laundering is closely linked to measures for combating organized crime, because effective protection against money laundering is an important tool in

---

[129] Article 20 law of 11 January 1993 to prevent using the financial system for money laundering. This law has been reviewed on several occasions, for example, by law of 12 January 2004. An appeal for annulment of the law of 2004 was brought before the Belgian Arbitragehof on 23 July 2004.

[130] Jean-Pierre Buyle, "Les avocats, auxiliaires de police," *Journ. Proc.* (2002), at 9; Ramon Mullerat, "Le secret professionnel dans la communauté européenne. Le secret professionnel de l'avocat en Espagne," in Edward Janssens & Jan Meerts (eds.), *Het beroepsgeheim van de advocaat in de Europese context* (Brussel, Larcier, 2003), at 159; Philip Traest, *supra* note 126, at 221.

[131] Philip Traest, *supra* note 126, at 221.

[132] David Morgan, "The threat to the professional secrecy of lawyers in Europe," in Edward Janssens & Jan Meerts (eds.), *supra* note 130, at 167-172.

[133] Philip Traest, *supra* note 126, at 232.

the fight against organized crime.

(a) European Union

In Joint Action 98/699/JHA of 3 December 1998 adopted by the Council on money laundering, the identification, tracing, freezing, seizing and confiscation of instrumentalities and the proceeds from crime, the member states agreed to make all serious offences, as defined in the Joint Action predicate, offences for the purpose of the criminalization of money laundering.[134] This Joint Action plan has now been partially repealed by the Framework Decision of 26 June 2001 on money laundering, the identification, tracing, freezing, seizing and confiscation of instrumentalities and the proceeds from crime.[135]

(b) Belgian Regulation

Money laundering is prohibited in the Belgian penal code.[136] A lawyer can be guilty of money laundering, which raises problems with regard to the very abstract and wide definition of money laundering in the Belgian penal code.

The disclosure in good faith by counsel to the president of the bar council, of which the lawyer concerned is a part, shall not constitute a breach of any restriction on disclosure of information imposed by contract or by any legislative, regulatory or administrative provision.[137] This Belgian provision gives rise to uncertainty as to what extent it provides immunity[138] from prosecution for the money laundering

---

[134] Joint Action of 3 December 1998 adopted by the Council on the basis of Article K.3 of the Treaty on European Union, on money laundering, the identification, tracing, freezing, seizing and confiscation of instrumentalities and the proceeds from crime, *O.J.* 9 December 1998, L 333/1.

[135] Council Framework Decision of 26 June 2001 on money laundering, the identification, tracing, freezing, seizing, and confiscation of instrumentalities and the proceeds from crime, *O.J.* July 5, 2001, L 182/1.

[136] Article 505 Belgian Penal Code.

[137] Article 20 law of 11 January 1993 to prevent using the financial system for money laundering.

[138] The concept of immunity has been used in Memorie van Toelichting, *Parl. St.* nr. 383/1

itself.[139] Moreover, there is no regulation concerning the problem of payment of counsel through means of illegally obtained money.

4.2.2.2.3.3 Fight Against Sexual Abuse of Minors: Belgian Penal Code

In the post-Dutroux era, the possibility of breaching professional secrecy was introduced into the Belgian penal code in 2000. Thus, counsel has the right – not the obligation – to report sexual offences on minors to the public prosecutor, when the victim has confided in defense counsel, there is a serious and imminent danger for the physical and psychological integrity of the involved minor and he cannot protect this integrity by himself or with the help of others.[140] This last condition clearly proves the *ultimum remedium* character of the right to report.[141] With regard to the fact that the Belgian penal code does not state that there is an obligation to report, but a mere right to do so, there is a mere breach, but not a violation of professional secrecy. Nevertheless, this legislative intervention reflects strengthening pressure on the professional confidentiality of lawyers in the last few years.

5. CONCLUSION

There is something very troubling in the fact that defense lawyers entrusted with the professional privilege of confidentiality now have an obligation to report unusual transactions possibly related to money laundering activities.

(Kamer 2003-2004).

[139] Filiep Deruyck, "Meester! Meester! Over de meldingsplicht van advocaten ter voorkoming van het witwassen van geld," *T. Strafr.* (2004), at 216; Philip Traest, *supra* note 126, at 227-228.

[140] Article 458 bis Belgian Penal Code.

[141] Vicky De Souter, "Het beroepsgeheim en de invoering van een spreekrecht door de wet van 28 november 2000 betreffende de strafrechtelijke bescherming van minderjarigen. Een nadere analyse van het artikel 458bis van het Strafwetboek," *T.J.K.* (2001), at 192.

This may result in over-reporting. There is a need for a fundamental discussion of the importance and meaning of the role and duties of counsel in criminal proceedings.

The current revival of the fight against (organized) crime has caused a certain polarization. Developments at the level of the European Union are almost solely aimed at the repressive side of criminal law, which shows that the interests of justice – in the conception of the interests of combating crime – take precedence over the concept of the autonomy of defense counsel.

The facilities and guarantees needed to practice the profession of criminal defense lawyer have been diminished in the fight against (organized) crime and terrorism. This international effort has been enhanced through national legislative measures, which may pose a real threat to legal protection. These European and domestic measures are twofold, including both the abstract and very broad definition of material penal provisions, which can be used by the public prosecutor to prosecute counsel, and vague and overbroad obligations to report.[142] Although the growth in organized crime and terrorism doubtlessly demands the introduction of appropriate measures, the autonomy of defense counsel should not be sacrificed for short-term gains.

Public authorities have an obligation to develop the procedural preconditions for effective legal assistance. The next logical step at the level of the European Union would be to develop a European charter for criminal defense lawyers, which should contribute to securing the right to a proper defense in criminal proceedings. The tasks and responsibilities of the criminal defense lawyers must form a consistent whole with the principles underlying the European Convention on the Protection of Human Rights and Fundamental

---

[142] Theo A. De Roos, "De ethiek van de raadsman in strafzaken," *Advocatenblad* (1995), at 159-64; Taru Spronken, *surpa* note 11, at 166-190.

Freedoms as elaborated by the Strasbourg court.[143] The European bars and professional organizations of criminal defense lawyers should respond to the European Union initiatives and give them greater substance and practical utility.[144]

---

[143] Taru Spronken, *supra* note 11, at 649-651; Taru Spronken, *supra* note 1, at 4.

[144] *Cf.* Recommendation Rec (2000) 21 of the Committee of Ministers to member states on the freedom of exercise of the profession of lawyer, adopted by the Committee of Ministers on 25 October 2000, cm.coe.int/ta/rec/2000/word/2000r21.doc: Bar associations or other lawyers' professional associations should draw up professional standards and codes of conduct and should ensure that, in defending the legitimate rights and interests of their clients, lawyers have a duty to act independently, diligently and fairly; Taru Spronken, *supra* note 1, at 13.

Checks and Balances in the Law of International Organizations

Jan Klabbers

In the spring of 2006, a political discussion of sorts arose within the European Forest Institute (EFI), a fairly small but highly atypical international organization devoted to forestry research and headquartered in Joensuu, Finland.[1] The EFI, set up in its present form in 2003, aimed to establish a branch office in one of its member states, and the inevitable question arose: which of the organs is competent to make that decision? Should that be the plenary body, in which all member states are represented? Or, would a decision by the executive organ be sufficient? Should it be the both of them acting together? Or could it be either one, acting autonomously? In other words: what role does autonomy play in relations between organs of an international organization, and to what extent do checks and balances exist governing those relations?

There has been little, if any, systematic attention to the notion of autonomy in the law of international organizations. This should not come as a surprise: traditionally, the law of international organizations has been dominated by a functionalist approach, which has proved highly instrumental in analyzing what organizations do and why they do it. Functionalism has, however, been less helpful in trying to come to terms with international organizations as political

---

[1] The organization is atypical in that apart from regular member states, it counts well over 100 research associations as associate or affiliated members. Indeed, EFI started out in 1993 as a research venture under Finnish law, only to be transformed into an intergovernmental organization in 2003. At the time of writing (spring 2006), it has 11 member states.

actors: issues of institutional autonomy, of control, of checks and balances, have remained under-illuminated.[2] The recent trend towards discerning some form of constitutionalism in international law generally as well as within international organizations does little to remedy this. Its main focus still rests on organizations as harbingers or guarantors of community values, acting beyond politics,[3] whereas a proper constitutionalist approach would have to start with the realization that organizations are, first and foremost, political actors.[4]

In the absence of a well-developed constitutionalist approach to international organizations, literature analyzing issues of powers or control is scarce. There is some literature on the relationship between organizations and their member states, both in general[5] and on more specific issues such as the transfer or delegation of powers by members to the organization,[6] or the control by the organization of member-state acts.[7] This literature suggests that autonomy is only

---

[2] *See* Jan Klabbers, "Introduction," in Jan Klabbers (ed.), *International Organizations* (Aldershot: Ashgate, 2005): xi-xxv.

[3] One of the more vocal protagonists of this type of constitutionalism is Erika de Wet, "The International Constitutional Order," 55 *International and Comparative Law Quarterly* (2006): 51-76.

[4] For a critique, *see* Jan Klabbers, "Constitutionalism Lite," 1 *International Organizations Law Review* (2004): 31-58.

[5] *See* Jan Klabbers, *An Introduction to International Institutional Law* (Cambridge: Cambridge University Press, 2002). *See also* Karel Wellens, *Remedies against International Organisations* (Cambridge: Cambridge University Press, 2002).

[6] *See* in particular Dan Sarooshi, *The United Nations and the Development of Collective Security: The Delegation by the UN Security Council of its Chapter VII Powers* (Oxford: Oxford University Press, 1999); Dan Sarooshi, *International Organizations and their Exercise of Sovereign Powers* (Oxford: Oxford University Press, 2005).

[7] *See* Niels M. Blokker, "Is the Authorization Authorized? Powers and practice of the UN Security Council to Authorize then Use of Force by 'Coalitions of the Able and Willing,'" 11 *European Journal of International Law* (2000): 541-568; *see also* Niels M. Blokker, "International Organizations and Their Members," 1 *International Organizations Law Review* (2004): 139-161.

partly present: typically, member-state autonomy must compete with the notion of cooperation for its place in the sun; organizational autonomy must compete with member-state autonomy.

The law of international organizations, however, comprises more than only the relations between organizations and their member states. It also covers relations between various international organizations, something largely left unexplored in the literature and hardly systematically addressed by case law,[8] despite various opportunities to do so. Thus, one might argue that the debate on whether the European Union should respect the European Convention on Human Rights, emanating from the Council of Europe, is in part concerned with the relationship between two different organizations;[9] by the same token, NATO's actions to end ethnic cleansing in Kosovo, despite the absence of Security Council approval, may be re-cast as a dispute on the precise relationship between the UN and NATO; and the already infamous decisions of the EU's Court of First Instance in cases concerning decisions of Security Council Sanctions Committees involves, in one way or another, the connection between the UN and the EU.[10]

One might also think of the unfortunate saga concerning the AIDS crisis as involving inter-organizational relationships.[11] On one view, the AIDS crisis is regarded as a trade

---

[8] *But see, Legality of the Use by a State of Nuclear Weapons in Armed Conflict*, advisory opinion, [1996] ICJ Reports 66, esp. para. 26 (in which the ICJ suggested that the tasks of the World Health Organization had to be analyzed in light of its being part of a larger group of international organizations).

[9] Possibly the best study (unhelpfully written in Dutch though) remains Rick Lawson, *Het EVRM en de Europese Gemeenschappen* (Deventer: Kluwer, 1999).

[10] *See* cases T-306/01, *Yusuf & Al Barakaat v. Council & Commission*, and T-315/01, *Kadi v. Council & Commission*, decisions of 21 September 2005, available at http://curia.eu.int. A first brief comment is Ramses A. Wessel, "The UN, the EU and *Jus Cogens*," 3 *International Organizations Law Review* (2006): 1-6.

[11] *See* Andreas Fischer-Lescano & Gunther Teubner, "Regime-Collisions: The Vain Search for

issue, involving the WTO and its TRIPS agreement. On another, it may be construed as a health issue, thus involving the WHO. On yet another view, the AIDS crisis may be recast as a human rights issue or even as a security issue,[12] opening the door for involvement of various other UN bodies. And things become more complicated still if one wants to do justice to the role of NGOs and transnational business groups or lobbies, having their own relationships with international organizations.

One may also analyze and discuss the relations between an organization and its staff in terms of autonomy. Staff members are supposed to be loyal to the organization only and not to their states of nationality, and any attempts by states to influence staff members of their nationality is usually frowned upon, as when Mussolini aspired to vet all Italian international civil servants. Yet, an episode such as the *Bustani* case, which concerned the dismissal of the administrative head of the Organization for the Prohibition of Chemical Weapons and ended up before the International Labour Organisation Administrative Tribunal a few years ago, illustrates just how difficult it may be to disentangle loyalties here, both those of the individual staff members and those of other actors.[13]

This paper will focus on a different, but equally neglected aspect of autonomy in international organizations: the relationship between various organs of the same organization. The emphasis here will be on the United Nations system, because the UN is the most important international organization, and because there is some (sparse) case law

---

Legal Unity in the Fragmentation of Global Law," 25 *Michigan Journal of International Law* (2004): 999-1046.

[12] The UN Security Council has included references to AIDS in its various peacekeeping resolutions. *See* Linda Fasulo, *An Insider's Guide to the UN* (New Haven: Yale University Press, 2004), 46.

[13] For further discussion, *see* Jan Klabbers, "Constitutionalism in Disguise? The Bustani Case Before the ILOAT," 53 *International and Comparative Law Quarterly* (2004): 455-464.

available from the International Court of Justice (ICJ).[14] My interest at present lies not in comprehensiveness or completeness, but in trying to flesh out a framework for analysis.

1. AUTONOMY WITHIN ORGANIZATIONS

Autonomy is usually taken to be a great good. Within states, autonomy is often advocated as a means of doing justice to the special position of special groups, and indeed, much law is based on the notion of the individual as an autonomous unit, as autonomy taps into widespread liberal values about self-determination, self-development and democracy. Yet, autonomy is limited by at least two considerations. The first of these is that as a value, autonomy meets its opposite in equally valued notions of solidarity and cooperation. Autonomy may be a good thing, but it (practically) cannot and (normatively) should not result in autarchy. Autonomy may be great, but should be wary of lapsing into unilateralism.[15]

This is intimately related to the second consideration: the autonomy of entity A, if taken too far, will encroach on the autonomy of entity B. This holds true in interpersonal relations (the neighbor wishing to exercise her autonomy by playing the trumpet all day long is bound to encroach on the autonomy of the neighbor aiming to study algebra);[16] it holds

---

[14] This has not been done all too often: the standard textbooks tend to discuss the organs of the UN followed by a functional analysis of its activities, rather than applying the more constitutionalist approach adopted in this paper. Examples include Bengt Broms, *The United Nations* (Helsinki: Suomalainen Tiedeakatemia, 1990); Benedetto Conforti, *The Law and Practice of the United Nations* (The Hague: Kluwer, 1997); and H.G. Nicholas, *The United Nations as a Political Institution* (3d ed., Oxford: Oxford University Press, 1967).

[15] But, for a spirited defense of US unilateralism, *see* Jed Rubenfeld, "Unilateralism and Constitutionalism," 79 *New York University Law Review* (2004): 1971-2028. Incidentally, Rubenfeld's unilateralism is defended by means of an appeal to values (in particular democracy), which renders it a species of the same genus as value-based constitutionalism – which he is less excited about.

[16] The example is derived from Ronald Dworkin, *Law's Empire* (London: Fontana, 1986), 293.

true in relations between states (thus giving rise to what Friedmann felicitously referred to as the international law of coexistence),[17] and holds equally true in intra-organizational relations.

The constitutional laws of states typically recognize this interplay between notions of autonomy and cooperation. Typically, a constitution will spell out not just what organs make up the state, but also how those organs relate to each other. It will, in familiar terms, create checks and balances between the various organs, or establish something of an "institutional balance"[18] between the various branches of government. Something similar could have been expected with the founding treaties of international organizations. After all, they too are supposed, like domestic constitutions, to sketch the contours of a political community, if not of citizens then at least of member states (and sometimes, arguably, both, as with the EU). They too, like domestic constitutions, create organs—indeed, the creation of at least one such organ is often considered one of the defining hallmarks of a proper international organization.[19] Moreover, the founding documents of international organizations are often even referred to as "constitutions," at least in common parlance.

Yet, the analogy has its limits: it turns out, on closer scrutiny, that the constitutions of international organizations will typically create one or more organs, but will not all that often specify the precise relationship between those organs. In most cases, the nature of that relationship can be derived from the different tasks given to the different organs;

---

[17] *See* Wolfgang Friedmann, *The Changing Structure of International Law* (New York 1964).

[18] The European Court of Justice already launched the idea of an "institutional balance" in one of its first decisions. *See* Case 9/56, *Meroni and others v. High Authority*, [1957-58] European Court Reports 133.

[19] *See generally* Henry G. Schermers & Niels M. Blokker, *International Institutional Law* (4th ed, Leiden: Martinus Nijhoff, 2003).

the relationship between organs may, so to speak, be implied from the constituent document. Besides, often enough, there might be no need to specify any particular relationship, as the tasks of organ A may not interfere with the tasks of organ B.

Still, as the following will suggest, there are many occasions where such overlapping tasks may occur or, conversely, tasks may be identified for which no organ has been appointed. The classic example can be seen in the law of treaties: under Article 20, paragraph 3, of the Vienna Convention on the Law of Treaties, adjudging the permissibility of a reservation made to the constituent document is the prerogative of what Article 20 refers to as the "competent organ" of the organization. Yet, few if any constituent documents actually designate an organ as "competent" in these matters, thus creating ample space for uncertainty and political argument.[20]

2. RELATIONS AMONG NON-JUDICIAL ORGANS OF THE UNITED NATIONS

The UN Charter contains a handful of references to inter-organ relations, but these are neither comprehensive nor systematic. Most well-known perhaps is that on some issues, the Security Council and the General Assembly are expected to work in tandem: one cannot act without the other. In a general sense, this holds true for many actions of the Security Council: as soon as the Council proposes something that costs money, the Council needs the Assembly's cooperation, as the Assembly holds the power of the purse (Article 17). A celebrated recent example involves the creation of the Yugoslavia Tribunal, endowed with only minimal funding in its early days, due to the Assembly's lack of enthusiasm

---

[20] The seminal study is Maurice Mendelson, "Reservations to the Constitutions of International Organizations," 45 *British Yearbook of International Law* (1971): 137-171.

concerning the creation of the Tribunal.[21]

Aside from its general budgetary power, however, there is little to suggest that the Assembly, under the Charter, has the ability to control the Council, and even the budgetary power may be circumvented by creating special budgets for special operations, as is generally the case with peace-keeping. At most, the Assembly may make recommendations to the Council relating to any matter under the Charter (Articles 10, 11 and 14), except where the Council is exercising its functions in relation to a concrete dispute or situation (Article 12), and the Assembly may bring matters to the attention of the Council (Article 11, paragraph 3). Moreover, the Council shall report annually to the Assembly, but without this entailing the possibility for the Assembly to censure the Council.[22]

There are other provisions of the Charter in which some form of relationship between various organs is envisaged. Most explicit perhaps (though not most lucid) is Article 60, which specifies that responsibility for the carrying out of the social-economic functions of the UN "shall be vested in the General Assembly and, under the authority of the General Assembly, in the Economic and Social Council." Other provisions confirm that the Economic and Social Council is subordinate to the General Assembly. Thus, agreements with specialized agencies are subject to approval by the Assembly (Article 63), and the Council shall perform such functions "as may be assigned to it by the General Assembly" (Article 66, paragraph 3).

Likewise, the Trusteeship Council was largely deemed subordinate to the General Assembly (except for strategic areas, with respect to which supervision would rest, under

---

[21] The story is well told in Gary Jonathan Bass, *Stay the Hand of Vengeance: The Politics of War Crimes Tribunals* (Princeton: Princeton University Press, 2000), 221-222.

[22] The composition of the Council is in part determined by the Assembly, which would give the Assembly, in theory, the power to use Council elections as rewards for good behavior. In practice, however, it does not quite seem to work that way.

Articles 83 and 85, with the Security Council): Article 87 paints a picture of the Trusteeship Council working under the authority of the General Assembly, while Article 88 specifies that the Trusteeship Council shall report to the Assembly.

Relations with the two remaining principal organs are different in nature. There is, in essence, no hierarchical relationship between the various political organs and the ICJ written into the Charter. The Charter merely provides that the Security Council has a role to play in the enforcement of ICJ decisions, while the General Assembly is authorized (and may authorize others) to request advisory opinions. There is (famously) no explicit provision on judicial review, and attempts to write judicial review into the Charter were defeated in 1945.[23]

Different in nature also are the provisions concerning the Secretariat and the role of the Secretary-General. The Secretary-General works, in a sense, in the service of four of the five principal organs (Article 98, appropriately, does not mention the ICJ). If there is a sense of hierarchy, it is in the relationship between Secretary-General and General Assembly, in that the Secretary-General is appointed by the General Assembly (Article 97), shall annually report to the Assembly (Article 98), and that staff regulations shall be established by the Assembly (Article 101).

The most interesting provisions of the Charter, for present purposes, are those sketching a relationship between the General Assembly and the Security Council, the two main political organs representing, respectively, the seemingly opposed notions of reflection and action.[24] As Martti Koskenniemi explains, the Assembly is the place where justice can be openly discussed, without anyone having to worry too much about any practical effects; the Council,

---

[23] *See* Section 3 below for further discussion.

[24] For an elaboration, *see* Jan Klabbers, "Two Concepts of International Organization," 2 *International Organizations Law Review* (2005): 277-293.

on the other hand, is where swift and decisive action can be taken so as to maintain or secure order in international affairs, without necessarily taking considerations of justice into account.[25]

On several topics, the drafters' idea was to create something of an institutional balance, suggesting that the one could not act in the absence of the other and therewith maintain a precarious balance between plenary and (quasi) executive. This applies to appointments of officials (the Secretary-General under Article 97 and, under a complicated procedure) to appointments of judges at the ICJ (under its Statute), but it is especially on issues of membership of the UN that this institutional balance is struck. The General Assembly has the final say about the admission of new member states and the suspension and expulsion[26] of those who are already member states (Articles 4, 5 and 6), subject however to recommendations by the Security Council. This should not come as a surprise: any attempt to establish a political community will have to find ways to define those who belong, and those who do not. Therefore, rules and procedures on membership assume enormous importance, and it makes sense to vest powers of admission and expulsion in the plenary and executive organs together.

While Articles 5 and 6 have largely led a dormant existence, Article 4 was the subject of litigation before the ICJ—not just once, but twice. Most relevant for present purposes was the second of these occasions, the *Second Admissions* case, an advisory opinion rendered in 1950. Faced with an internally divided Security Council, paralyzed over the admission of states sympathetic to the East and West in the late 1940s,

---

[25] Martti Koskenniemi, "The Police in the Temple: Order, Justice and the UN: A Dialectical View," 6 *European Journal of International Law* (1995): 325-348.

[26] *See* on the latter generally Nagendra Singh, *Termination of Membership of International Organisations* (London : Stevens & Sons, 1958); and Konstantinos Magliveras, *Exclusion from Participation in International Organisations: The Law and Practice behind Member States' Expulsion and Suspension of Membership* (The Hague: Kluwer, 1999).

the General Assembly started to wonder whether, under paragraph 2 of Article 4, a Security Council recommendation was really necessary. After all, a common reading of the word "recommendation" would attest to its non-binding nature, and if non-binding, one might as well do without.

The Court, however, disagreed, and did so in terms of what may well be construed as an institutional balance. In the Court's view, the way the UN Charter was drafted made clear that the drafters intended decisions of this sort to be the province of the two organs together: plenary and executive were supposed to work in tandem, and failing the participation of one of them, the tandem could not function. As the Court put it in unequivocal terms: "...the recommendation of the Security Council is the condition precedent to the decision of the Assembly by which the admission is effected."[27]

It is perhaps useful to spell out that the Court sought (and found) its answer in what it held to be the wishes of the founding fathers of the UN, treating the matter by and large as one of treaty interpretation following the maxim that the ordinary meaning of the text ought normally to be followed. The Court found support for its interpretation in what it called the "structure" of the Charter, under which neither organ was subordinate to the other, nor the earlier practice of Council and Assembly: "The organs to which Article 4 entrusts the judgment of the organization in matters of admission have consistently interpreted the text in the sense that the General Assembly can decide to admit only on the basis of a recommendation of the Security Council."[28]

This approach, if generally applied, carries some risks. As Judge Sir Percy Spender pointed out in his separate opinion to *Certain Expenses*, one cannot without something more to support the argument equate the practice of organs with the

---

[27] *See Competence of the General Assembly for the Admission of a State to the United Nations,* Advisory Opinion, [1950] ICJ Reports 4, at 8.

[28] *Id.* at 9.

practice of parties to an agreement. It is, in other words, by no means self-evident that the conduct of the organs of an organization ought to be considered as subsequent practice of the parties for purposes of treaty interpretation; much less can the practice of the organ, without more, be seen as providing evidence of the intentions of the drafters. This may work well with parties' subsequent conduct under bilateral treaties, but is bound to be less plausible when the practice of organs is concerned.[29]

Sir Percy's opinion is characteristic of the ambivalence with which international lawyers typically treat international organizations.[30] On the one hand, his words can be seen as taking the organization seriously in its own right: the organ is independent, and cannot be reduced to the aggregate of the member states composing it, or composing the organization at large. On the other hand, however, this is precisely how he eventually defended his position:

> [T]he inescapable reality is that both the General Assembly and the Security Council are but the mechanisms through which the members of the United Nations express their views and act. The fact that they act through such an organ, where a majority prevails and so determines the practice, cannot, it seems to me, give any greater probative value to the practice established within that organ than it would have as conduct of the Members that comprise the majority if pursued outside of that organ.[31]

---

[29] See *Certain Expenses of the United Nations* (Article 17, Paragraph 2, of the Charter), Advisory Opinion, [1962] ICJ Reports 151, Spender J. concurring, at 190. Judge Fitzmaurice, in his separate opinion, seems to hint at similar concerns, without being very specific. *See id.*, Fitzmaurice J. concurring, at 201.

[30] *See generally* Klabbers, *An Introduction*, note 5 above.

[31] *Certain Expenses*, note 29 above, Spender J. concurring, at 192. It is perhaps worth observing that when it comes to the creation of customary international law, the Court usually (if not invariably) treats organizational practice as cumulative state practice. *See further* Jan Klabbers,

A more general conclusion to draw from *Admissions II*, given the way the Court treated the matter as one involving the interpretation of a particular treaty, is that there may hardly be any general rules or principles of international institutional law. The point is, of course, that institutions are not only independent, separate entities, but are also, first and foremost perhaps, the creations of states, and these states, sovereign as they are still deemed to be, are capable of creating each and every institutional structure they can possibly think of. While a comparative survey may reveal common patterns amongst organizations, a court (or any court) will have to take the specific desires of the organization's founders into account.

The relationship between the General Assembly and the Security Council came to be discussed anew in *Certain Expenses*. Here, spurred by the argument that the member states could not be expected to pay the UN's expenses which would flow from *ultra vires* decisions of the UN's organs, the Court found a balance of sorts in the idea that the Charter did not create any hierarchy between the two organs, other than the background rule that authorizing enforcement action is the sole prerogative of the Security Council.[32] And more systematically, the Court reached the conclusion that as far as the legality of the acts of organs of the organization are concerned, in the absence of any mechanism for doing so in the Charter, "each organ must, in the first place at least, determine its own jurisdiction."[33] Moreover, given the broad purposes of the UN, it was not lightly to be expected that activities taken by the UN would be *ultra vires* with regard to the role of the organization itself. Activities might possibly be

---

"International Organizations in the Formation of Customary International Law," in Enzo Cannizzaro & Paolo Palchetti (eds.), *Customary International Law and the Use of Force: A Methodological Approach* (Leiden: Martinus Nijhoff, 2005), 179-195.

[32] *Certain Expenses*, note 29 above, at 162-165.

[33] *Id.* at 168. The ICJ resorted to this more recently in its *WHA* opinion, note 8 above.

ultra vires with respect to the particular organ taking them, but that would not without more affect their legality, as both under domestic and international law, it is possible that "the body corporate or politic may be bound, as to third parties, by an *ultra vires* act of an agent."[34]

Whereas all this could be interpreted as the Court somehow siding with the General Assembly (given that the complaint resulting in the advisory opinion had involved the suggestion that the Assembly had appropriated powers properly resting with the Council), the Court made sure not to wander off too far in the Assembly's company. The idea that the Assembly's budgetary power would give the Assembly the edge in its relations with the UN's other principal organs was dispelled: under reference to the earlier *Effect of Awards* opinion, the Court held that the budgetary power did not amount to an absolute power to approve or disapprove the acts of the other organs: whenever other organs incur costs, the Assembly, exercising its budgetary power, has no choice but to honor such commitments.[35]

Somewhat between the lines, the relationship between the General Assembly and the Security Council was also discussed in the 1971 *Namibia* opinion. After the General Assembly had terminated South Africa's mandate over South West Africa, it had to look to the Security Council for help in enforcement, as the Assembly itself lacked the clout to convince South Africa to withdraw. The Security Council did indeed become involved, but the Court made sure to underline that the Council's involvement stemmed from its own powers: those relating to the maintenance of international peace and security.[36] In other words: it was not a case of one organ telling

---

[34] *Id.* at 168 (italics in original – JK).

[35] *Id.* at 169.

[36] *See Legal Consequences for States of the Continued Presence of South Africa in Namibia* (South West Africa) notwithstanding *Security Council Resolution 276* (1970), Advisory Opinion, [1971] ICJ Reports 16, at 51-52.

the other what to do; instead, both operated and co-operated, on the basis of their own proper powers.[37]

The political risk involved in this approach will be obvious: there might be instances in which the two organs cannot speak with one voice. What if the Security Council refuses to act, perhaps due to the veto of one of the great powers? Or, what if the Council had been satisfied that a partial South African withdrawal would be sufficient to restore peace and security, but such partial withdrawal would not, as such, be the result the Assembly would have liked to see? Or, to what extent can the Assembly really be considered autonomous if it is dependent on the Council for enforcement?[38] Would it have been conceivable for the Assembly to terminate the mandate without first ensuring itself of the assistance of the Council? It is here that the autonomy of organs of an organization runs the risk of becoming either counterproductive or a mere chimera.

3. RELATIONS AMONG NON-JUDICIAL ORGANS AND JUDICIAL ORGANS OF THE UNITED NATIONS

While generally the autonomy of organs seems to be taken for granted and considered as a great good, things are different when it comes to relations with judicial organs or sub-organs. Two different situations may be envisaged. First, when a non-judicial organ makes judicial or quasi-judicial determinations, it appropriates (at least temporarily) a power belonging to a different organ. This has sometimes come up in the relevant

---

[37] As Judge Fitzmaurice pithily put it: "...if the Assembly's resolution 2145 lacked *in se* validity and legal effect [as he held to be the case – JK], no amount of 'confirmation' by the Security Council could validate it or lend it such effect, or independently bring about the revocation of a mandate." *See Namibia*, note 36 above, Fitzmaurice J. dissenting, at 291.

[38] Judge Padilla Nervo hit a nerve when (inadvertently, one presumes) he put it as follows: "To the extent that General Assembly resolution 2145 (XXI) may be considered a recommendation to the Security Council, it became fully effective upon its endorsement by the Council." *See id.*, Padilla Nervo J. concurring, at 114.

cases, but never been dealt with in any great detail. Thus, in the *Namibia* case, South Africa argued that in finding that South Africa had violated the terms of its mandate, the General Assembly was exercising a judicial function for which it lacked the competence.

The Court's response was somewhat elliptic: referring to the infamous 1966 decision in *South West Africa* (by which Liberia and Ethiopia were denied standing to sue South Africa for violating the mandate), the Court held that it would be "inconsistent" to deny the right to act to the political organs most closely involved, and would, moreover, "amount to a complete denial of the remedies available against fundamental breaches of an international undertaking."[39] Presumably, what the Court meant to stipulate was that if the Court cannot intervene due to states lacking standing, then surely someone else must have the power to intervene. That is, of course, a plausible approach, but one not based on traditional powers doctrine, but rather arrived at by default.

Second, the relationship between judicial and other organs is usually cast in terms of judicial review: does the judicial organ have the power to correct, halt, and perhaps even invalidate the acts of the political organs? Judicial review of UN acts by the ICJ is a highly explosive, controversial topic, with the antagonists occupying one of two extreme positions. On the one hand, there are those who feel that since the UN is supposed to be a legal community, it stands to reason that in such a community the legal acts of political organs could potentially be submitted to judicial scrutiny. After all, the politicians may get it wrong (and arguably often enough do get it wrong), so judicial review would offer the possibility of a corrective.

Others, however, suggest that even if this were desirable, reality dictates that political organs carry political responsibilities. If these can be handled in accordance with

---

[39] *Id.* at 49.

the law, so much the better; but there might be times when developing, or boldly interpreting, or perhaps even departing from, the law is necessary for the maintenance of peace and security (e.g. in the fight against terrorism). In such cases, to insist on judicial review, while running the risk that the political organs will all but ignore judicial verdicts, can only undermine the legitimacy of the entire system: to introduce judicial review under such conditions might do more harm than good to peace and security—and to international law.[40]

The ICJ itself has always been tiptoeing through this political minefield. In *Certain Expenses*, the Court seemed to hold that whatever it might have been seen to be doing, it was most assuredly not engaged in judicial review: it referred to the fact that proposals to give the Court the ultimate say in matters of Charter interpretation had been rejected, and emphasized that the opinion it was giving was an advisory opinion.[41] And in *Namibia*, the Court put it fairly explicitly: "Undoubtedly, the Court does not possess powers of judicial review or appeal in respect of the decisions taken by the United Nations organs concerned."[42]

Yet, notwithstanding these remonstrations, the Court did leave the door open for at least some judicial review. The wording in *Namibia* already provides something of an indication: by referring to the "decisions taken by the United Nations organs concerned," the Court limited its statement to the case at hand or, at most, to decisions of the Council and Assembly generally. It did not, however, close the door completely; it did not say that it lacked the power of review "in respect of decisions of United Nations organs."

---

[40] For a discussion, with references, *see* Jan Klabbers, "Straddling Law and Politics: Judicial Review in International Law," in R. St. J. MacDonald & D.M. Johnston (eds.), *Towards World Constitutionalism* (Leiden: Martinus Nijhoff, 2005), 809-835.

[41] *Certain Expenses*, note 29 above, at 168.

[42] *Namibia*, note 36 above, at 45, para. 89.

One setting in which the Court seems to have accepted judicial review (or at least not to have rejected the possibility) is the setting in which the validity or legality of decisions does not form the central legal question, but arises incidentally. It already hinted at this distinction in *Namibia*: the Court felt that it had to consider objections to the legality or validity of decisions before it was able to determine the legal consequences of those decisions.[43]

Similarly, the ICJ kept the door ajar for review of Security Council resolutions in its 1992 order in *Lockerbie*, pointing out that while, *prima facie,* those resolutions would have to be accepted and carried out by the UN's membership, the Court was not at that stage of the proceedings "called upon to determine definitively the legal effect" of the resolution concerned.[44] Likewise, in one of its *Bosnia* orders, the Court suggested that an analysis of the merits, including judicial review of Security Council acts, would fall outside the proper scope of a request for interim measures of protection.[45] As *ad hoc* Judge Lauterpacht explained in his separate opinion, "... the Court, as the principal judicial organ of the United Nations is entitled, indeed bound, to ensure the rule of law within the United Nations system and, in cases properly brought before it, to insist on adherence by all United Nations organs to the rules governing their operation."[46] Still, he was careful to point out that such judicial review would have its limits:

---

[43] *Id.*

[44] See *Case Concerning Questions of Interpretation and Application of the 1971 Montreal Convention Arising from the Aerial Incident at Lockerbie (Libyan Arab Jamahiriya v United States of America)*, [1993] ICJ Reports 114, at 126, paras. 42-43. And a few paragraphs later, the Court repeated that in dealing with Libya's request for interim measures of protection, "the Court is not called upon to determine any of the other questions which have been raised before it in the present proceedings...." *Id.* at para. 45.

[45] See *Case Concerning Application of the Convention on the Prevention and Punishment of the Crime of Genocide (Bosnia and Herzegovina v Yugoslavia (Serbia and Montenegro))*, Order of 13 IX 1993, [1993] ICJ Reports 325, at 344-345, paras. 40-41.

[46] *Id.*, Lauterpacht J. concurring, at 439, para. 99.

"...it does not embrace any right of the Court to substitute its discretion for that of the Security Council in determining the existence of a threat to the peace, a breach of the peace or an act of aggression, or the political steps to be taken following such a determination."[47]

It thus seems well-established that the ICJ is entitled, perhaps even bound, to exercise a certain degree of judicial review over acts of the Security Council in two kinds of situations. The first, as exemplified in the *Lockerbie* and the *Bosnia* orders, is when a Security Council act is of relevance to the determination of the rights and obligations of states in disputes between two states.[48] Second, it would seem that the Court allows itself incidental review of the legality of a Security Council act, also in the setting of an advisory opinion, if this is necessary for a proper determination of the rights and obligations of UN member states; this latter setting will be less obvious, as requests for advisory opinions typically (or ideally, perhaps) address the legal position of international institutions rather than of states. Still, as much can be derived from the *Namibia* opinion.[49]

Indeed, in this latter, strictly institutional setting, the Court seems to have no doubts about the power of judicial review.[50] As early as 1954, in *Effect of Awards*, the Court analyzed whether the General Assembly had the power to establish

---

[47] *Id.*

[48] *See also* James Crawford, "*Marbury v. Madison* at the International Level," 36 *George Washington International Law Review* (2004): 505-514.

[49] I have argued elsewhere that there seems to be no solid reason to limit review to Security Council acts; in principle, all binding acts of all UN organs could be susceptible to the above-mentioned (limited) form of review. *See* Klabbers, *Straddling Law and Politics*, note 40 above.

[50] Actually, there might be yet a different setting, but one that is not terribly exciting. The Court may derive the power to review another's decision from a legal text. For instance, in its UNESCO judgment, it could have found the power to review the validity of judgments of the Administrative Tribunal of the ILO on the tribunal's Statute, which explicitly conferred such a power on the ICJ. *See Judgments of the Administrative Tribunal of the International Labour Organisation upon Complaints made against the United Nations Educational, Scientific and Cultural Organization*, Advisory Opinion, [1956] ICJ Reports 77.

a United Nations Administrative Tribunal (UNAT), without first asking whether this could be called judicial review. It could be argued that the Court only addressed the issue after already answering the question before it (which was the question whether the General Assembly could refuse to give effect to UNAT awards of compensation), but even so, it is telling that the Court seems absolutely unconcerned with the propriety of reviewing the legality of a General Assembly act. Nor is there any discussion of this point in the separate and dissenting opinions.[51] The question seems not to have been considered to be in dispute.

The question whether the Court can review the acts of organs of organizations other than the UN has met with a similar response. This was addressed, and by implication answered affirmatively, in the *IMCO Maritime Safety Committee* opinion. The Court was called upon, as it put it, to appreciate whether in composing its Maritime Safety Committee as it had, the Assembly of the Inter-Governmental Maritime Consultative Organization had complied with Article 28 of IMCO's constituent document.[52] The Court happily proceeded to do precisely that, without standing still to wonder whether such an exercise of judicial review of the act of an organ of an international organization was properly within its province.[53] As in *Effect of Awards*, the possibility of judicial review appears not to have been an issue, despite having been raised in some of the written statements submitted to the Court.[54]

---

[51] See *Effect of Awards of Compensation made by the United Nations Administrative Tribunal*, Advisory Opinion, [1954] ICJ Reports 47, at 56-57.

[52] See *Constitution of the Maritime Safety Committee of the Inter-Governmental Maritime Consultative Organization*, Advisory Opinion, [1960] ICJ Reports 150.

[53] Neither did the two dissenting opinions (by Judges Klaestad and Moreno Quintana) question the propriety of review.

[54] See, e.g., the written statement of the government of Liberia (arguing in favor of judicial review), in *IMCO Maritime Safety Committee* (note 52 above), Pleadings, Oral Arguments, Documents, at 78-79.

Alternatively, one could suggest that in both cases, the issue was conceived not so much as one of judicial review, but rather as simply a matter of treaty interpretation in the abstract (what is the proper interpretation of the word "elected" in IMCO's constituent document?), without this leading to a determination of legality or otherwise by the Court itself. There is some support for this reading in the pleadings,[55] and indeed the Court seems to have regarded the issue as one of treaty interpretation and therewith automatically falling within the scope of its advisory jurisdiction.[56]

4. CONCLUSION

The present brief survey suggests that there are few, if any, general rules in international institutional law concerning checks and balances. Partly, this may be a variation perhaps on James Madison's "melancholy reflection"[57] that no government would be necessary if men were angels.[58] International organizations were, for a long time, supposed to do only good, be angelic in nature, and thus checks and

---

[55] Including the support of the UK, which was in favor of maintaining the original decision and thus not overly keen on seeing it reviewed. *See, e.g,* the written statement of the government of the United Kingdom (*id* at 234-235), as well as the oral presentation by the UK's representative, Mr. Francis Vallat (*id.* at 371).

[56] Whether a subtle distinction between interpretation and review is workable depends, to some extent, on the underlying conception of review. Those who feel that review includes the power to invalidate might be more inclined to accept the distinction than those who feel that review might precede invalidation, but can also take place without it. *See further* on such and related issues, Klabbers, *Straddling Law and Politics*, note 40 above.

[57] The characterization is Arendt's. *See* Hannah Arendt, "The End of Tradition," in Hannah Arendt, *The Promise of Politics* (New York: Schocken, 2005, Jerome Kohn ed.), 81-92, at 85.

[58] "But what is government itself but the greatest of all reflections on human nature? If men were angels, no government would be necessary. If angels were to govern men, neither external nor internal controuls [sic] on government would be necessary." *See* James Madison, "The Federalist No. 51," in Alexander Hamilton, James Madison and John Jay, *The Federalist Papers* (New York: Bantam Books, 1982, Gary Wills ed., first published 1781-1782), 261-265, at 262.

balances were hardly even discussed.[59] And where in the
UN system checks and balances do exist, they seem to be
balances rather than checks: the various political organs
are supposed not so much to control each other, as to act in
concert, as when they admit new member states or appoint
the next Secretary-General. As discussed above, the case-law
of the ICJ points in the same direction.

This survey of UN rules and ICJ practice suggests that there
is some room for judicial review over the acts of UN organs.
In particular, in situations not directly affecting the rights
or obligations of member states, but rather affecting the
position of the UN organs in respect to each other,[60] the ICJ
has not been shy to accept requests for review. It has been
more reluctant to do so when rights or obligations of member
states are at stake, but even in those situations the ICJ has
retained the possibility of judicial intervention.

The law of international organizations, traditionally, has
been dominated by a functionalist perspective. With the
dawning realization that international organizations actually can do wrong, comes the realization that the law and
thinking about the law, could usefully help to develop a
constitutional perspective. Such a perspective, however,
should not be constitutional in the sense of embodying
higher community values. There is, after all, ample reason
to be skeptical about claims about community values: as
Schmitt once put it, "whoever invokes humanity wants to
cheat."[61] Instead, it might be more productive to develop

---

[59] *See* Jan Klabbers, "The Changing Image of International Organizations," in Jean-Marc
Coicaud & Veijo Heiskanen (eds.), *The Legitimacy of International Organizations* (Tokyo:
United Nations University Press, 2001), 221-255. *See also* José E. Alvarez, "International
Organizations: Then and Now," 100 *American Journal of International Law* (2006): 324-347.

[60] Needless to say, the precise dividing line between issues relating merely to intra-organ
relations and issues affecting the rights and obligations of member states is impossible to draw
with any degree of precision. Yet, rough as it is, it does seem a useful starting point for further
reflection.

[61] *See* Carl Schmitt, *The Concept of the Political* (Chicago: University of Chicago Press, 1996,

constitutionalism as a more modest, control-oriented, approach to international organizations, while respecting the autonomy of those organizations, their organs, and their member states alike.

George Schwab ed.), 54.

Index

abortion, 20,27,37-8,47-8,50-1
  for minors, 37-8
  rates, 35-6
Advocates General, 76,82,83,86,90
aggression, 159
AIDS, 143-4
Alaska, 36,38
American Convention on Human Rights, 105-8
  Art. 8, 107-8
American University, ix
Amsterdam Treaty, 102
Arizona, 34
Arkansas, 32,33,34,36
assisted suicide, *see* suicide, assisted
authority,
  horizontal, 91
  judicial, 73-96
  vertical, 91
autonomy, *passim*
  constraints on, 3,6
  death and, 7-8,55-72
  defined, 1
  family, 11-53
  group, 4-6
  in selecting institutions, 42-51
  institutional, 142
  mistakes about, 6
  moral, 3
  of clients, 62
  of defense counsel, 97-139
  of criminals, 56,71
  of international organizations, 141-63
  personal, 4
  state, 49
  to be executed, 57-8
  value of, 1-9,49
  within organizations, 145-7

morality,
  fundamental, 16,
  regulation of, 15,16-22
  sexual, *see* sexual morality
Murphy, Jane, 24-5,28
Murphy, Jeffrie, 18
Murray v. United Kingdom, 109
Mussolini, Benito, 144

Namibia, 154,156,158,159
Netherlands, Kingdom of the, 58,59,60,61,64,69,73
neutrality, 11,16,69-70
Nevada, 34,38
New Hampshire, 32,34,38
New Jersey, 32,33,36,38,41
New Mexico, 32,34,38,41
New York, 32,33,35-6,38,41
Nikula v. Finland, 118-20
Nock, Steven L., 30-1
North Atlantic Treaty Organization, 143
North Dakota, 34,38
Nozick, Robert, 44-5,45-6,48

Öcalan, Abdullah, 101
Öcalan v. Turkey, 101,110-1
Oklahoma, 32,33
oppression, 4,6,52
  defined, 5
Oregon, 38,58,60
Organization for Economic Cooperation and Development, 128
organizations, international, *see* international organizations
organized crime, 128-37,138
overlapping consensus, 42

passion, 3
peace,
  threat to, 159
Pederzoli, Patrizia, 79
Pennsylvania, 34,35
People v. Lavalle, 63,64
Perruche, Nicolas, 74,92,96
Pilkerton, Thomas III, ix
Plato, 78,93

moral, 23-4
Van Gend and Loos, 84
Vermont, 34,36,38,41
Vienna Action Plan, 130,131
Vienna Convention on the Law of Treaties, 147
  Art. 20, 147
virtue, 43
  family, 25

Wahl, Catherine, ix
Washington, 35,36,38
Webster, Ryan, ix
welfare, 5
Wendt-Taczac, Cheri, ix
Wilcox, W. Bradford, 30-1
will, 5
women, 26,27-8
World Trade Organization, 144
Wurthrow, Robert, 29
Wyoming, 32,34,35,41